Sound

TEACHER'S GUIDE

SCIENCE AND TECHNOLOGY FOR CHILDREN

NATIONAL SCIENCE RESOURCES CENTER
Smithsonian Institution • National Academy of Sciences
Arts and Industries Building, Room 1201
Washington, DC 20560

NSRC

The National Science Resources Center is operated by the Smithsonian Institution and the National Academy of Sciences to improve the teaching of science in the nation's schools. The NSRC collects and disseminates information about exemplary teaching resources, develops and disseminates curriculum materials, and sponsors outreach activities, specifically in the areas of leadership development and technical assistance, to help school districts develop and sustain hands-on science programs.

STC Project Supporters

National Science Foundation
Smithsonian Institution
U.S. Department of Defense
U.S. Department of Education
John D. and Catherine T. MacArthur Foundation
The Dow Chemical Company Foundation
E. I. du Pont de Nemours & Company
Amoco Foundation, Inc.
Hewlett-Packard Company
Smithsonian Institution Educational Outreach Fund
Smithsonian Women's Committee

This project was supported, in part,
by the
National Science Foundation
Opinions expressed are those of the authors
and not necessarily those of the Foundation

ISBN 0-89278-744-9

Published by Carolina Biological Supply Company, 2700 York Road, Burlington, NC 27215.
Call toll free 1-800-334-5551.

This material is based upon work supported by the National Science Foundation under Grant No. ESI-9252947. Any opinions, findings, and conclusions or recommendations expressed in this material are those of the author(s) and do not necessarily reflect the views of the National Science Foundation.

CB787129805

Foreword

Since 1988, the National Science Resources Center (NSRC) has been developing Science and Technology for Children (STC), an innovative hands-on science program for children in grades one through six. The 24 units of the STC program, four for each grade level, are designed to provide all students with stimulating experiences in the life, earth, and physical sciences and technology while simultaneously developing their critical-thinking and problem-solving skills.

Sequence of STC Units

Grade	Life, Earth, and Physical Sciences and Technology			
1	Organisms	Weather	Solids and Liquids	Comparing and Measuring
2	The Life Cycle of Butterflies	Soils	Changes	Balancing and Weighing
3	Plant Growth and Development	Rocks and Minerals	Chemical Tests	Sound
4	Animal Studies	Land and Water	Electric Circuits	Motion and Design
5	Microworlds	Ecosystems	Food Chemistry	Floating and Sinking
6	Experiments with Plants	Measuring Time	Magnets and Motors	The Technology of Paper

The STC units provide children with the opportunity to learn age-appropriate concepts and skills and to acquire scientific attitudes and habits of mind. In the primary grades, children begin their study of science by observing, measuring, and identifying properties. Then they move on through a progression of experiences that culminate in grade six with the design of controlled experiments.

Sequence of Development of Scientific Reasoning Skills

Scientific Reasoning Skills	Grades					
	1	2	3	4	5	6
Observing, Measuring, and Identifying Properties	◆	◆	◆	◆	◆	◆
Seeking Evidence Recognizing Patterns and Cycles		◆	◆	◆	◆	◆
Identifying Cause and Effect Extending the Senses				◆	◆	◆
Designing and Conducting Controlled Experiments						◆

The "Focus-Explore-Reflect-Apply" learning cycle incorporated into the STC units is based on research findings about children's learning. These findings indicate that knowledge is actively constructed by each learner and that children learn science best in a hands-on experimental environment where they can make their own discoveries. The steps of the learning cycle are as follows:

- Focus: Explore and clarify the ideas that children already have about the topic.

- Explore: Enable children to engage in hands-on explorations of the objects, organisms, and science phenomena to be investigated.

- Reflect: Encourage children to discuss their observations and to reconcile their ideas.

- Apply: Help children discuss and apply their new ideas in new situations.

The learning cycle in STC units gives students opportunities to develop increased understanding of important scientific concepts and to develop positive attitudes toward science.

The STC units provide teachers with a variety of strategies with which to assess student learning. The STC units also offer teachers opportunities to link the teaching of science with the development of skills in mathematics, language arts, and social studies. In addition, the STC units encourage the use of cooperative learning to help students develop the valuable skill of working together.

In the extensive research and development process used with all STC units, scientists and educators, including experienced elementary school teachers, act as consultants to teacher-developers, who research, trial teach, and write the units. The process begins with the developer researching the unit's content and pedagogy. Then, before writing the unit, the developer trial teaches lessons in public school classrooms in the metropolitan Washington, D.C., area. Once a unit is written, the NSRC evaluates its effectiveness with children by field-testing it nationally in ethnically diverse urban, rural, and suburban public schools. At the field-testing stage, the assessment sections in each unit are also evaluated by the Program Evaluation and Research Group of Lesley College, located in Cambridge, Mass. The final editions of the units reflect the incorporation of teacher and student field-test feedback and of comments on accuracy and soundness from the leading scientists and science educators who serve on the STC Advisory Panel.

The STC project would not have been possible without the generous support of numerous federal agencies, private foundations, and corporations. Supporters include the National Science Foundation, the Smithsonian Institution, the U.S. Department of Defense, the U.S. Department of Education, the John D. and Catherine T. MacArthur Foundation, the Dow Chemical Company Foundation, the Amoco Foundation, Inc., E. I. du Pont de Nemours & Company, the Hewlett-Packard Company, the Smithsonian Institution Educational Outreach Fund, and the Smithsonian Women's Committee.

Acknowledgments

David Hartney was the primary researcher and developer of the *Sound* unit. The field-test edition of *Sound* was edited by Marilyn Fenichel and illustrated by Max-Karl Winkler. The unit was trial taught in Shirley Tyler's third-grade classroom at Long Branch Elementary School in Arlington, Virginia. Following national field-testing, *Sound* was revised by Joyce Lowry Weiskopf, STC project director (1992–95), and Douglas Lapp, NSRC executive director, with Dorothy Sawicki as editor. Max-Karl Winkler illustrated this final edition.

Other NSRC staff who contributed to the development of this unit include Charles N. Hardy, NSRC deputy director for information dissemination, materials development, and publications (1995–96); Sally Goetz Shuler, deputy director for development, external relations, and outreach; Dean Trackman, publications director; Heidi M. Kupke, publications technology specialist; and Theodore Schultz, program officer for networking (1992–96). The formative evaluation of *Sound* was carried out by Sabra Lee, senior research associate, Program Evaluation and Research Group, Lesley College. Additional field-testing of the unit was completed in Patricia Moriarity's third-grade classroom at King's Park Elementary School in Fairfax County, Virginia.

The technical and educational review of *Sound* was conducted by:

Albert V. Baez, President, Vivamos Mejor/USA, Greenbrae, CA

Robert E. Gibbs, Professor of Physics, Eastern Washington University, Cheney, WA

Jayne L. Hart, Professor of Biology, George Mason University, Fairfax, VA

Sarah Koenig, Science Teacher, Washington Episcopal School, Bethesda, MD

Herbert S. Lin, Senior Program Officer, Computer Science and Telecommunications Board, National Academy of Sciences, Washington, DC

Sue Livers, Teacher, Willson Science and Technology School, Bozeman, MT

Randy McGinnis, Assistant Professor of Science Education, Science Teaching Center, Department of Curriculum and Instruction, University of Maryland at College Park, College Park, MD

Jerome Pine, Professor of Physics, California Institute of Technology, Pasadena, CA

Emily VanZee, Assistant Professor of Science Education, Science Teaching Center, Department of Curriculum and Instruction, University of Maryland at College Park, College Park, MD

The NSRC would like to thank the following individuals and school systems for their assistance with the national field-testing of the unit:

Huntsville City School System, Huntsville, AL
Coordinator: Judy Kirk, Huntsville City Schools
Ginnie Forney, Teacher, Morris Elementary School
Karen Thomas, Teacher, Morris Elementary School
Coordinator: Teresa Rollings, Madison County Schools
Rahonda Everett, Teacher, Central School
Betsy Woods, Teacher, Central School

Antioch Unified School District, Antioch, CA
Coordinator: Christine Williams, Supervisor, K–12 Education
MaryLou Blomberg, Teacher, Bidwell Elementary School
Kathy Carademos, Teacher, Marsh Elementary School
Lynn Haywood, Teacher, Fremont Elementary School

The School District of Kansas City, Kansas City, MO
Coordinator: Bruce Evans, Science/Technology Coordinator
Tracy Costello, Teacher, Blenheim Elementary School
Laura Powell, Teacher, West Rock Creek Elementary School
Doug Wilson, Teacher, North Rock Creek/Korte Academy of Environmental Science, Independence, MO

Elkhart Community Schools, Elkhart, IN
Coordinator: Eugene W. Hungate, Assistant Director, Curriculum and Instruction
Mary Ann Surface, Teacher, Osolo Elementary School
Kathleen Thies, Teacher, Hawthorne Elementary School
Ron Wolschlager, Teacher, Osolo Elementary School

The NSRC would also like to thank the following individuals for their contributions to the unit:

Bill Badders, Teacher, Cleveland Public Schools, Cleveland, OH

L. J. Benton, Coordinator, Instructional Materials Processing Center, Fairfax County Public Schools, Fairfax, VA

William Brown, Director, Eli Whitney Museum, Hamden, CT

David Burgevin, Photographic Production Control, Office of Printing, Imaging, and Photographic Services, Smithsonian Institution, Washington, DC

Katherine Darke, STC Program Assistant (1993–95)

Debbie Deal, Curriculum Developer, Fairfax, VA

JoAnn DeMaria, Teacher, Hutchison Elementary School, Herndon, VA

Bernard Finn, Curator, Division of Electricity and Modern Physics, National Museum of American History, Smithsonian Institution, Washington, DC

Mary Florentine, Professor of Audiology, Northeastern University, Boston, MA

Jack Goldstein, Professor of Physics, Brandeis University, Waltham, MA

David Green, Director of Technology, Durham County Schools, Durham, NC

Martha Green, Teacher, Bethesda Elementary School, Durham, NC

Joe Griffith, Director, Hands-on Science Center, Science in American Life, National Museum of American History, Smithsonian Institution, Washington, DC

Andrew Harriger, Wilma Crall Elementary School, Galion, OH

Ben Harriger, Wilma Crall Elementary School, Galion, OH

Donna Hartney, Ernst & Young, Cleveland, OH

Sheldon Hochheiser, Senior Research Associate, AT&T Archives, Short Hills, NJ

Michael Howard, Director, Science Education Programs, Kentucky Science and Technology Council, Inc., Lexington, KY

Audrey Humphries, Teacher, Watkins School, Capitol Hill Cluster Schools, Washington, DC

Teri Johnston, Teacher, Hybla Valley Elementary School, Alexandria, VA

Cliff Malcolm, Curriculum Corporation, Victoria, Australia

Mary Ellen McCaffrey, Photographic Production Control, Office of Imaging, Printing, and Photographic Services, Smithsonian Institution, Washington, DC

Patricia McGlashan, Consultant, Stoney Creek, CT

Dane Penland, Chief, Imaging and Technology Services Branch, Office of Imaging, Printing, and Photographic Services, Smithsonian Institution, Washington, DC

Sarah Rauber, Office Manager, The Bicultural Center, Riverdale, MD

Miguel Savage, Science Education Consultant, African Forum for Children's Literacy and Science and Technology, Nairobi, Kenya

Elliot Sivowitch, Museum Specialist, Division of Electricity and Modern Physics, National Museum of American History, Smithsonian Institution, Washington, DC

Daniel Steinel, Information Service Manager, Music Educators National Conference, Reston, VA

Robert Allen Strawn, Photographer, Arlington, VA

Jeff Tinsley, Chief, Special Assignments/Photography Branch, Office of Imaging, Printing, and Photographic Services, Smithsonian Institution, Washington, DC

Margery Tracy, Principal, Long Branch Elementary School, Arlington, VA

Ellie Uehling, Teacher, Wakefield Forest Elementary School, Fairfax, VA

Rick Vargas, Photographer, Office of Imaging, Printing, and Photographic Services, Smithsonian Institution, Washington, DC

Susan Williamson, Head Librarian, The Annenberg School for Communication, University of Pennsylvania, Philadelphia, PA

The librarians and staff of the Central Reference Service, Smithsonian Institution Libraries

Douglas Lapp
Executive Director
National Science Resources Center

STC Advisory Panel

Peter P. Afflerbach, Professor, National Reading Research Center, University of Maryland, College Park, MD

David Babcock, Director, Board of Cooperative Educational Services, Second Supervisory District, Monroe-Orleans Counties, Spencerport, NY

Judi Backman, Math/Science Coordinator, Highline Public Schools, Seattle, WA

Albert V. Baez, President, Vivamos Mejor/USA, Greenbrae, CA

Andrew R. Barron, Professor of Chemistry and Material Science, Department of Chemistry, Rice University, Houston, TX

DeAnna Banks Beane, Project Director, YouthALIVE, Association of Science-Technology Centers, Washington, DC

Audrey Champagne, Professor of Chemistry and Education, and Chair, Educational Theory and Practice, School of Education, State University of New York at Albany, Albany, NY

Sally Crissman, Faculty Member, Lower School, Shady Hill School, Cambridge, MA

Gregory Crosby, National Program Leader, U.S. Department of Agriculture Extension Service/4-H, Washington, DC

JoAnn E. DeMaria, Teacher, Hutchison Elementary School, Herndon, VA

Hubert M. Dyasi, Director, The Workshop Center, City College School of Education (The City University of New York), New York, NY

Timothy H. Goldsmith, Professor of Biology, Yale University, New Haven, CT

Patricia Jacobberger Jellison, Geologist, National Air and Space Museum, Smithsonian Institution, Washington, DC

Patricia Lauber, Author, Weston, CT

John Layman, Professor of Education and Physics, University of Maryland, College Park, MD

Sally Love, Museum Specialist, National Museum of Natural History, Smithsonian Institution, Washington, DC

Phyllis R. Marcuccio, Associate Executive Director for Publications, National Science Teachers Association, Arlington, VA

Lynn Margulis, Professor of Biology, Department of Botany, University of Massachusetts, Amherst, MA

Margo A. Mastropieri, Co-Director, Mainstreaming Handicapped Students in Science Project, Purdue University, West Lafayette, IN

Richard McQueen, Teacher/Learning Manager, Alpha High School, Gresham, OR

Alan Mehler, Professor, Department of Biochemistry and Molecular Science, College of Medicine, Howard University, Washington, DC

Philip Morrison, Professor of Physics Emeritus, Massachusetts Institute of Technology, Cambridge, MA

Phylis Morrison, Educational Consultant, Cambridge, MA

Fran Nankin, Editor, *SuperScience Red,* Scholastic, New York, NY

Harold Pratt, Senior Program Officer, Development of National Science Education Standards Project, National Academy of Sciences, Washington, DC

Wayne E. Ransom, Program Director, Informal Science Education Program, National Science Foundation, Washington, DC

David Reuther, Editor-in-Chief and Senior Vice President, William Morrow Books, New York, NY

Robert Ridky, Associate Professor of Geology, University of Maryland, College Park, MD

F. James Rutherford, Chief Education Officer and Director, Project 2061, American Association for the Advancement of Science, Washington, DC

David Savage, Assistant Principal, Rolling Terrace Elementary School, Montgomery County Public Schools, Rockville, MD

Thomas E. Scruggs, Co-Director, Mainstreaming Handicapped Students in Science Project, Purdue University, West Lafayette, IN

Larry Small, Science/Health Coordinator, Schaumburg School District 54, Schaumburg, IL

Michelle Smith, Publications Director, Office of Elementary and Secondary Education, Smithsonian Institution, Washington, DC

Susan Sprague, Director of Science and Social Studies, Mesa Public Schools, Mesa, AZ

Arthur Sussman, Director, Far West Regional Consortium for Science and Mathematics, Far West Laboratory, San Francisco, CA

Emma Walton, Program Director, Presidential Awards, National Science Foundation, Washington, DC, and Past President, National Science Supervisors Association

Paul H. Williams, Director, Center for Biology Education, and Professor, Department of Plant Pathology, University of Wisconsin, Madison, WI

Contents

Goals for *Sound*

In this unit, students investigate the phenomenon of sound. Their experiences introduce them to the following concepts, skills, and attitudes.

Concepts

- Sounds are produced by vibrating objects and vibrating columns of air.

- Pitch and volume are two characteristics of sound.

- Changing the way an object vibrates can change the pitch and volume of the sound produced.

- Pitch is determined by the frequency of the vibrations; volume is determined by the amplitude of the vibrations.

- Changing the length, tension, or thickness of a string affects the frequency of vibration and, therefore, the pitch of the sound produced.

- The human ear has a membrane that vibrates when sound reaches it; the ear and the brain translate these vibrations into the sensation of sound.

- Sound is produced by the human vocal cords as air moves through the tightened cords.

Skills

- Performing experiments with sound.

- Describing the results of investigations with sound.

- Comparing and discussing the volume and pitch of the sounds produced.

- Communicating results through writing and with graphs.

- Reflecting on experiences with sound through writing and discussion.

- Using the results of previous experiments with sound to predict outcomes in new situations.

- Applying previously learned concepts and skills to design new sound-producing devices.

- Reading to obtain more information about sound, hearing, and the vocal cords.

Attitudes

- Developing an interest in investigating sound.

- Recognizing the importance of hearing safety.

Unit Overview and Materials List

How can children study sound? They can't see it. They can't touch it. But they do ask questions about it. What causes different sounds? How does a guitar work? Why do some sounds hurt my ears? *Sound,* an 8-week, 16-lesson unit for third-grade students, provides a series of activities to help children discover answers to these and other questions they may have about sound.

In the first half of the unit, students explore some basic principles about how sound is produced, how sound travels, and how the frequency of vibrations is related to pitch. They begin by producing sounds with different-sized tuning forks in Lesson 1, discussing the similarities and differences in what they hear. In Lesson 2, they explore how the sounds produced by the tuning forks travel through different materials. The concept that sound is produced by vibrations is reinforced in Lesson 3, when students explore the sounds made by vibrating nails of different sizes.

Lessons 4 and 5 focus on the length of a vibrating object as a specific variable that can affect the pitch of the sound produced. As students change the length of the vibrating part of a ruler, they closely watch the frequency of the vibrations and carefully listen to the corresponding changes in pitch. Discussing the relationship between the length of the vibrating part of the ruler, the vibrations observed, and the resulting pitch introduces the concept that higher pitches result from higher frequencies of vibration.

Students' explorations of varying the pitch of a vibrating ruler lead to their investigation of ways to change the pitch of vibrations that cannot be seen. In Lesson 6, students experiment with the sound produced by the vibrating column of air in a slide whistle. In the embedded assessment in Lesson 7, students design and demonstrate a wind instrument that uses a vibrating reed. This gives them the opportunity to reflect on and apply what they have learned about the relationship between the length of a vibrating column of air and the pitch of the sound produced.

As they begin the second half of the unit, students first focus on the eardrum. In Lesson 8, they make a model eardrum and observe how sounds make it vibrate, just as sounds make a real eardrum vibrate. This experience reinforces children's earlier investigations into how sound travels through different substances. A reading selection at the end of Lesson 8 highlights the importance of hearing safety.

Lessons 9 through 12 engage students in an in-depth exploration of the variables that affect the pitch of a sound produced by a vibrating string. Using a harplike instrument, they observe that changing the tension or the length of a string changes its pitch. Students then observe that strings with the same length and tension but different thicknesses produce sounds of different pitches. In Lesson 13, students focus on factors affecting volume, or loudness of the sounds produced, as they add a bridge to their harps.

In Lesson 14, students investigate the sound-producing "instrument" that enables them to speak, sing, or shout—the human vocal cords. They discover how the observations they have made about vibrating strings also apply to the sounds produced by this organ of the human body. The unit concludes in Lessons 15 and 16 with students designing and constructing a musical instrument or other device to demonstrate what they have learned about sound.

In this unit, not only do students find answers to their questions about sound, but they can begin to appreciate the consistency of the principles they have discovered. This reinforcement continues throughout the unit as they experiment with various devices and make connections between what they hear and what they can observe. Recording results with simple charts and diagrams as well as with words and pictures in their science notebooks enables students to review the results of their previous work and to make connections between what they learn in different investigations.

Materials List

Below is a list of the materials needed for the *Sound* unit. Please note that the metric and English equivalent measurements in this unit are approximate.

- 1   *Sound* Teacher's Guide
- 15   *Sound* Student Activity Books
- 8   large tuning forks (low pitch)
- 8   small tuning forks (high pitch)
- 30   plastic trays
- 1   roll of heavy-duty aluminum foil
- 15   pieces of convoluted foam-rubber sponge, 10 × 15 cm (4 × 6 in)
- 15   steel nails, 12D
- 15   steel nails, 20D
- 15   steel nails, 40D
- 30   plastic rulers with centimeter scale, 30 cm (12 in) long
- 16   whistle mouthpieces
- 16   plastic tubes, 15-mm (⅝-in) diameter, 10.5 cm (4¼ in) long
- 16   squeeze bulbs
- 16   wooden dowels, 14-mm (⁹⁄₁₆-in) diameter, 15 cm (6 in) long
- 45   plastic cups, 284 ml (10 oz)
- 250   plastic "Jumbo" drinking straws, 20 cm (7¾ in) long
- 200   plastic "Super-Jumbo" drinking straws (in diameter, slightly larger than the "Jumbo"), 20 cm (7¾ in) long
- 8   hole punches
- 15   sheets of thin latex rubber, 15 cm (6 in) square
- 15   noisemakers
- 1   spool of 20-lb nylon fishing line
- 30   pieces of cardboard, 3 × 5 cm (1¼ × 2 in)
- 30   plastic cups, 261 ml (9 oz), squat
- 150   small steel washers, No. 10, 12-mm (½-in) diameter
- 60   eyebolts, 3.75 cm (1½ in) long, with 4-mm (³⁄₁₆-in) diameter
- 60   wing nuts to fit eyebolts

- 15   pegboards, 15 × 45 × 0.6 cm (6 × 18 × ¼ in), with holes slightly larger than 4-mm (³⁄₁₆-in) diameter, to fit eyebolts
- 1   spool of 8-lb nylon fishing line
- 1   spool of 30-lb nylon fishing line
- 1   spool of 50-lb nylon fishing line
- 1   spool of 60-lb nylon fishing line
- 15   wooden bridges for pegboard harps, 2.5 × 15 × 0.65 cm (1 × 6 × ⁵⁄₁₆ in)
- 30   rubber bands, No. 33
- 30   rubber bands, No. 64

- *   Newsprint or poster board
- *   Colored markers
- *30   unsharpened pencils
- *8   heavy hardback books, about 2.5 cm (1 in) thick
- *   String (heavy cotton or nylon twine)
- *   Table salt
- *   Fine sand
- *   Masking tape
- *   Miscellaneous objects such as shoe boxes, milk cartons, clay flowerpots, rubber bands, string, plastic food trays, cardboard tubes, jar lids
- *   Scissors
- *   Paper clips
- *   Candle (self-standing, or in candlestick)
- *   Matches
- *   Glue or paste
- **8   wooden metersticks, yardsticks, or similar pieces of wood, 1 m (39 in) long

*Note: These items are not included in the kit. They are available in most schools or can be brought from home.

**Note: Metersticks or yardsticks are not included in the kit because most schools have them on hand. Yardsticks can be purchased at a hardware or home supply store, or metersticks can be ordered from Carolina Biological Supply Company (800-334-5551).

Teaching *Sound*

The following information on unit structure, teaching strategies, materials, and assessment will help you give students the guidance they need to make the most of their hands-on experiences with this unit.

Unit Structure

How Lessons Are Organized in the Teacher's Guide: Each lesson in the *Sound* Teacher's Guide provides you with a brief overview, lesson objectives, key background information, a materials list, advance preparation instructions, step-by-step procedures, and helpful management tips. Many of the lessons include recommended guidelines for assessment. Lessons also frequently indicate opportunities for curriculum integration. Look for the following icons that highlight extension ideas:

Please note that all record sheets, blackline masters, student instructions, and reading selections may be copied and used in conjunction with the teaching of this unit.

Student Activity Book: The *Sound* Student Activity Book accompanies the Teacher's Guide. Written specifically for students, this activity book contains simple instructions and illustrations to enable students to conduct the activities in this unit. The Student Activity Book will help students follow along with you as you guide each lesson. It will also provide guidance for students who may miss a lesson or for those who do not immediately grasp certain activities or concepts. In addition to previewing each lesson in the Teacher's Guide, you may find it helpful to preview the accompanying lesson in the Student Activity Book.

The lessons in the Student Activity Book are divided into the following sections, paralleling the

Teacher's Guide:

- **Think and Wonder** sketches for students a general picture of the ideas and activities of the lesson described in the **Overview and Objectives** of the Teacher's Guide.

- **Materials** lists the materials students and their partners or teammates will be using.

- **Find Out for Yourself** flows in tandem with the steps in the **Procedure** and **Final Activities** sections of the Teacher's Guide and briefly and simply walks students through the lesson's activities.

- **Ideas to Explore,** which frequently echoes many of the activities in the **Extensions** section in the Teacher's Guide, gives students additional activities to try out or ideas to think about.

Teaching Strategies

Classroom Discussion: Class discussions, effectively led by the teacher, are important vehicles for science learning. Research shows that the way questions are asked, as well as the time allowed for responses, can contribute to the quality of the discussion.

When you ask questions, think about what you want to achieve in the ensuing discussion. For example, open-ended questions, for which there is no one right answer, will encourage students to give creative and thoughtful answers. You can use other types of questions to encourage students to see specific relationships and contrasts or to help them summarize and draw conclusions. It is good practice to mix these questions. It also is good practice always to give students "wait time" before expecting them to answer; this will encourage broader participation and more thoughtful answers. You will want to monitor responses, looking for additional situations that invite students to formulate hypotheses, make generalizations, and explain how they arrived at a conclusion.

Brainstorming: Brainstorming is a whole-class exercise in which students contribute their thoughts about a particular idea or problem. When used to introduce a new science topic, it can be a stimulating and productive exercise. It also is a useful and efficient way for the teacher to find out what students know and think about a topic. As students learn the rules for brainstorming, they will become increasingly adept in their participation.

To begin a brainstorming session, define for students the topics about which they will share ideas. Explain the following rules to students:

- Accept all ideas without judgment.

- Do not criticize or make unnecessary comments about the contributions of others.

- Try to connect your ideas to the ideas of others.

Cooperative Learning Groups: One of the best ways to teach hands-on science is to arrange students in small groups. There are several advantages to this organization. It provides a small forum in which students can express their ideas and get feedback. It also offers students a chance to learn from one another by sharing ideas, discoveries, and skills. With coaching, students can develop important interpersonal skills that will serve them well in all aspects of life. As students work, they will often find it productive to talk about what they are doing, which results in a steady hum of conversation. If you or others in the school are accustomed to a quiet room, this busy atmosphere may require some adjustment.

Learning Centers: You can give supplemental science materials a permanent home in the classroom in a spot designated as the learning center. Students can use the center in a number of ways: as an "on your own" project center, as an observation post, as a trade-book reading nook, or simply as a place to spend unscheduled time when assignments are done. To keep interest in the center high, change the learning center or add to it often. Here are a few suggestions of items to include:

- Science trade books on sound, hearing, music, and famous scientists (see the Bibliography for suggested titles).

- A set of materials so that students can test other sounds produced.

- Articles about hearing safety and advertisements about hearing loss and hearing aids collected from magazines and newspapers.

- Information and posters about sign language.

Materials

Safety: This unit does not contain any dangerous materials, but common sense dictates that students exercise routine care with all materials. It is good practice to tell your students that, in science class, materials are never put in the mouth or ears. Students should also be reminded that certain items, such as rubber bands, rulers, nails, and straws, should be used only as directed.

Organization of Materials: To help ensure an orderly progression through the unit, you will need to establish a system for storing and distributing materials. Being prepared is the key to success. Here are a few suggestions:

- Read through the **Materials List** on pg. 4. Begin to collect the items you will need that are not provided in the kit.

- Organize your students so that they are involved in distributing and returning materials. If you have an existing network of cooperative groups, delegate the responsibility to one member of each group.

- Organize a distribution center and instruct your students to pick up and return supplies to that area. A cafeteria-style approach works especially well when there are large numbers of items to distribute.

- Look at each lesson in advance. Some have suggestions for handling materials.

- Management tips are provided. Look for this icon:

Assessment

Philosophy: In the Science and Technology for Children program, assessment is an ongoing, integral part of instruction. Because assessment emerges naturally from the activities in the lessons, students are assessed in the same manner in which they are taught. They may, for example, perform experiments, record their observations, or make oral presentations. Such assessments permit the examination of processes as well as of products, emphasizing what students know and can do.

The learning goals in STC units include a number of different science concepts, skills, and attitudes. Therefore, a number of different strategies are provided to help you assess and document your students' progress toward the goals. These strategies also will help you report to parents and appraise your own teaching. In addition, the assessments will enable your students to view their own progress, reflect on their learning, and formulate further questions for investigation and research.

Figure T-1 summarizes the goals and assessment strategies for this unit. The left-hand column lists the individual goals for the *Sound* unit and the lessons in which they are addressed. The right-hand column identifies lessons containing assessment sections to which you can turn for specific assessment strategies. These strategies are summarized as bulleted items.

Assessment Strategies: The assessment strategies in STC units fall into three categories: matched pre- and post-unit assessments, embedded assessments, and additional assessments.

The first lesson of each STC unit is a *pre-unit assessment.* It gives you information about what students already know about the unit's topic and what they want to find out. It often includes a brainstorming session during which students share their thoughts about the topic through exploring one or two basic questions. In the *post-unit assessment* following the final lesson, the class revisits the pre-unit assessment questions, giving you two sets of comparable data that indicate students' growth in knowledge and skills.

Throughout a unit, assessments are incorporated, or embedded, into lessons. These *embedded assessments* are activities that occur naturally within the context of both the individual lesson and the unit as a whole; they are often indistinguishable from instructional activities. By providing structured activities and guidelines for assessing students' progress and thinking, embedded assessments contribute to an ongoing, detailed profile of growth. In many STC units, the last lesson is an embedded assessment that challenges students to synthesize and apply concepts or skills from the unit.

Additional assessments can be used to determine students' understanding after the unit has been completed. In these assessments, students may work with materials to solve problems, conduct experiments, or interpret and organize data. In grades three through six, they may also complete self-assessments or paper-and-pencil tests. When you are selecting additional assessments, consider using more than one assessment to give students with different learning styles opportunities to express their knowledge and skills.

Documenting Student Performance: In STC units, assessment is based on your recorded observations, students' work products, and oral communication. All these documentation methods combine to give you a comprehensive picture of each student's growth.

Teachers' *observations and anecdotal notes* often provide the most useful information about students' understanding, especially in the early grades when some students are not yet writing their ideas fluently. Because it is important to document observations used for assessment, teachers frequently keep note cards, journals, or checklists. Many lessons include guidelines to help you focus your observations. The blackline master on pg. 11 provides a format you may want to use or adapt for recording observations. It includes this unit's goals for science concepts and skills.

Work products, which include both what students write and what they make, indicate students' progress toward the goals of the unit. Children produce a variety of written materials during a unit. Record sheets, which include written observations, drawings, graphs, tables, and charts, are an important part of all STC units. They provide evidence of each student's ability to collect, record, and process information. Students' science journals are another type of work product. Often a rich source of information for assessment, these journal writings reveal students' thoughts, ideas, and questions over time.

Students' written work products should be kept together in folders to document learning over the course of the unit. When students refer back to their work from previous lessons, they can reflect on their learning. In some cases, students do not write or draw well enough for their products to be used for assessment purposes, but their experiences do contribute to the development of scientific literacy.

Oral communication—what students say formally and informally in class and in individual sessions with you—is a particularly useful way to learn what students know. This unit provides your students with many opportunities to share and discuss their own ideas, observations, and opinions. Some young children may be experiencing such activities for the first time. Encourage students to participate in discussions, and stress that there are no right or wrong responses. Creating an environment in which students feel secure expressing their own ideas can stimulate rich and diverse discussions.

Individual and group presentations can give you insights about the meanings your students have assigned to procedures and concepts and about their confidence in their learning. In fact, a student's verbal description of a chart, experiment, or graph is frequently more useful for assessment than the product or results. Questions posed by other students following presentations provide yet another opportunity for you to gather information. Ongoing records of discussions and presentations should be a part of your documentation of students' learning.

Sound: Goals and Assessment Strategies

Concepts	
Goals	**Assessment Strategies**
Sounds are produced by vibrating objects and vibrating columns of air. Lessons 1–16	Lessons 1, 4, 7, 9, 14, 16, and Additional Assessments 1–3 ▪ Pre- and post-unit assessments ▪ Notebook entries ▪ Class brainstorming charts ▪ Class discussions ▪ Record sheets ▪ Student-made instruments ▪ Oral presentations ▪ Student self-assessment
Pitch and volume are two characteristics of sound. Lessons 1, 3–16	Lessons 1, 4, 7, 9, 16, and Additional Assessments 1–3 ▪ Pre- and post-unit assessments ▪ Notebook entries ▪ Record sheets ▪ Class discussions ▪ Student-made instruments ▪ Oral presentations
Changing the way an object vibrates can change the pitch and volume of the sound produced. Lessons 4–16	Lessons 4, 7, 9, 16 ▪ Notebook entries ▪ Record sheets ▪ Class discussions ▪ Student-made instruments ▪ Oral presentations
Pitch is determined by the frequency of the vibrations; volume is determined by the amplitude of the vibrations. Lessons 4–5, 9–13, 15–16	Lessons 4, 9, 16 ▪ Notebook entries ▪ Record sheets ▪ Student-made instruments ▪ Oral presentations
Changing the length, tension, and thickness of a string affects the frequency of vibration and, therefore, the pitch of the sound produced. Lessons 9–16	Lessons 9, 16 ▪ Notebook entries ▪ Class discussions ▪ Student-made instruments ▪ Oral presentations
The human ear has a membrane that vibrates when sound reaches it; the ear and the brain translate these vibrations into the sensation of sound. Lesson 8	Lesson 14 ▪ Notebook entries ▪ Class discussions ▪ Teacher observations
Sound is produced by the human vocal cords as air moves through the tightened cords. Lesson 14	Lesson 14 ▪ Notebook entries ▪ Class discussions ▪ Teacher observations

Skills	
Goals	**Assessment Strategies**

Performing experiments with sound.
    Lessons 1–16
	Lessons 1, 4, 7, 9, 14, 16, and Additional Assessment 2
	  ▪ Pre- and post-unit assessments
	  ▪ Notebook entries
	  ▪ Record sheets
	  ▪ Student-made instruments
	  ▪ Teacher observations

Describing the results of investigations with sound.
    Lessons 1–16
	Lessons 1, 4, 7, 9, 14, 16 and Additional Assessment 2
	  ▪ Pre- and post-unit assessments
	  ▪ Notebook entries
	  ▪ Record sheets
	  ▪ Class discussions
	  ▪ Oral presentations
	  ▪ Student self-assessment

Comparing and discussing the volume and pitch of the sounds produced.
    Lessons 1, 3–16
	Lessons 1, 4, 7, 9, 16, and Additional Assessment 2
	  ▪ Pre- and post-unit assessments
	  ▪ Notebook entries
	  ▪ Record sheets
	  ▪ Class discussions
	  ▪ Student-made instruments
	  ▪ Oral presentations

Communicating results through writing and with graphs.
    Lessons 1, 3–7, 9–16
	Lessons 1, 4, 7, 9, 14, 16, and Additional Assessment 2
	  ▪ Notebook entries
	  ▪ Record sheets

Reflecting on experiences with sound through writing and discussion.
    Lessons 1–16
	Lessons 1, 4, 7, 9, 14, 16, and Additional Assessments 1 and 3
	  ▪ Pre- and post-unit assessments
	  ▪ Notebook entries
	  ▪ Class brainstorming charts
	  ▪ Class discussions
	  ▪ Oral presentations
	  ▪ Teacher observations

Using the results of previous experiments with sound to predict outcomes in new situations.
    Lessons 3–4, 6–7, 15–16
	Lessons 4, 7, 9, 16
	  ▪ Notebook entries
	  ▪ Record sheets
	  ▪ Student-made instruments

Applying previously learned concepts and skills to design new sound-producing devices.
    Lessons 6–7, 15–16
	Lessons 7, 16
	  ▪ Notebook entries
	  ▪ Record sheets
	  ▪ Student-made instruments
	  ▪ Oral presentations
	  ▪ Teacher observations

Reading to obtain more information about sound, hearing, and the vocal cords.
    Lessons 4, 6, 8, 14
	Lesson 4
	  ▪ Notebook entries
	  ▪ Class discussions

Attitudes	
Goals	**Assessment Strategies**
Developing an interest in investigating sound. Lessons 1–16	Lessons 1, 4, 7, 9, 16, and Additional Assessments 1–3 ▪ Pre- and post-unit assessments ▪ Notebook entries ▪ Class discussions ▪ Oral presentations ▪ Teacher observations ▪ Student self-assessment
Recognizing the importance of hearing safety. Lesson 8	Lesson 14 ▪ Notebook entries ▪ Class discussions

Sound: Observations of Student Performance

STUDENT'S NAME:	
Concepts	**Observations**
• Sounds are produced by vibrating objects and vibrating columns of air.	
• Pitch and volume are two characteristics of sound.	
• Changing the way an object vibrates can change the pitch and volume of the sound produced.	
• Pitch is determined by the frequency of the vibrations; volume is determined by the amplitude of the vibrations.	
• Changing the length, tension, or thickness of a string affects the frequency of vibration and, therefore, the pitch of the sound produced.	
• The human ear has a membrane that vibrates when sound reaches it; the ear and the brain translate these vibrations into the sensation of sound.	
• Sound is produced by the human vocal cords as air moves through the tightened cords.	
Skills	
• Performing experiments with sound.	
• Describing the results of investigations with sound.	
• Comparing and discussing the volume and pitch of the sounds produced.	
• Communicating results through writing and with graphs.	
• Reflecting on experiences with sound through writing and discussion.	
• Using the results of previous experiments with sound to predict outcomes in new situations.	
• Applying previously learned concepts and skills to design new sound-producing devices.	
• Reading to obtain more information about sound, hearing, and the vocal cords.	

Thinking about Sound

Overview and Objectives

This first lesson serves both as an assessment of students' prior knowledge and as an introduction to the characteristics of sound. Through a brainstorming session, students begin to express their own ideas and to raise questions that reflect their current understanding of sound. Investigating the sounds produced by two different-sized tuning forks provides focus for further discussion and exploration of sound. These preliminary activities introduce a sequence of investigations into the nature of sound that continues through Lesson 7.

- Students set up a science notebook that they will use to record their ideas, questions, and observations.

- Students share their ideas and questions about sound.

- Students investigate and describe sounds produced by tuning forks.

- Students discuss and classify sounds they have heard.

Background

Throughout this unit, students will explore and describe the characteristics of sound. In doing so, they will come to understand a basic fact about sound: it is produced by vibrations. A **vibration** is a repeated back-and-forth motion. Sound vibrations are produced by musical instruments, such as drums or guitars, and by countless nonmusical sources—such as a car engine, rustling leaves, or a cricket rubbing its legs together. All sounds are caused by vibrations.

Very simply described, a vibrating object makes the air around it vibrate. These sound vibrations pass through the air to our ears, strike our eardrums, and cause them to vibrate. Bones in the middle ear then transfer the vibrations of the eardrum to the fluid-filled inner ear. The movement of the fluid in the inner ear causes hairlike nerve receptors in the inner ear to move. The movement of these receptors causes electrochemical signals to be generated and carried along the auditory nerve to the brain. The brain perceives these signals as sound.

Sounds have two important characteristics—pitch and volume. The **pitch** of a sound can be described by the words "low" or "high." Examples of low-pitched sounds are the rumble of a large truck or the bass notes of a pipe organ. High-pitched sounds include a bird's trill or the treble notes of a flute. The pitch of a sound is directly related to the frequency of vibration of the object producing the sound. The **frequency** is the number of times the back-and-forth movement occurs in a second.

Volume describes how loud or soft a sound is. Volume is directly related to the magnitude, or amplitude, of the back-and-forth movement of the vibrating object. Sound sources with large-amplitude vibrations set up sound vibrations of large amplitude in the air surrounding the source, and the listener perceives these vibrations as loud sounds. Understanding the difference between volume and pitch is sometimes a challenge for students.

As students work through each lesson, they will discover what they must do to make each sound and will learn how to describe a sound according to its pitch and volume. In later lessons, they will have the opportunity to discover that changing the way an object vibrates can change the kind of sound produced.

For example, a student can pluck a rubber band and the resulting sound will have a certain pitch; if the child stretches the rubber band tighter and plucks again, the sound will have a higher pitch. Students will find out that low-pitched sounds are caused by vibrations that are of low frequency, whereas high-pitched sounds are caused by higher-frequency vibrations.

To increase the volume of the sound produced by a rubber band or guitar string, a student can pull the rubber band or guitar string farther to the side before releasing it. This produces larger back-and-forth movements in the vibrating object, which increase the volume of the sound produced.

This unit is designed to increase students' understanding of sound; to develop their skills in observing, describing, and predicting; and to give them an opportunity to apply what they have learned to design new ways of creating sounds. The information in the **Background** sections will help the teacher focus students' observations and facilitate discussions. The use of correct terminology should *follow* students' explorations and grow from their own need to communicate experiences and ideas. Remember that the ability to memorize and spell technical terms does not indicate understanding.

In Lesson 1, each group of students will work with two different-sized tuning forks. The tuning forks produce distinctly different pitches; the larger one makes the lower-pitched sound. Depending on how hard the tuning fork is struck, the sound can be louder or softer. This lesson therefore provides an excellent opportunity for students to discuss what they already know about sound and to ask some questions about sound that they would like to investigate further during the unit.

Materials

For each student
   1   science notebook

For every two students
   1   *Sound* Student Activity Book

For every four students
   1   large tuning fork
   1   small tuning fork

For the class
   3   sheets of newsprint
   1   marker

Preparation

1. Arrange the class so that each student works with a partner in a group of four.

2. Prepare three charts to use during the brainstorming session and class discussions. Write one title at the top of each sheet of newsprint:

   ■ Sounds We Have Heard

   ■ Ways to Make Sounds

   ■ Questions We Have about Sound

3. Prepare one science notebook for each student. These can be spiral or bound notebooks with a pocket for loose papers. Pocket folders with three-hole fasteners also work well.

4. Review this lesson as it is presented in the Student Activity Book. Decide when you will distribute these books to the students.

5. Read the boxed information, "Tips on Using a Tuning Fork," on pg. 16, and experiment with the tuning forks before the lesson.

Procedure

1. Distribute a science notebook to each student. Ask students to write their names and the date on the first page. Discuss the use of the notebooks for recording ideas, observations, and questions, and stress the importance of dating each entry.

2. Refer to the class charts labeled "Sounds We Have Heard" and "Ways to Make Sounds." Challenge students to think about various sounds and how they think these sounds are made. Then ask them to write some of their ideas in their science notebooks.

3. Invite students to share their ideas about sounds and how they are made in a class brainstorming session. Record their ideas and questions on the first two charts. (See Figure 1-1.) Be sure to write the date on these charts for future reference.

Figure 1-1

Sample pre-unit assessment charts

SOUNDS WE HAVE HEARD

shouts
laughing
horns
cars
radios
teacher's voice
referee's whistle
dog's bark
bell

WAYS TO MAKE SOUNDS

talk
turn on TV
play CDs
clap hands
start the car
slam the door
ring a bell
scratch the chalkboard
play your trumpet

Tips on Using a Tuning Fork

A tuning fork is a device made of metal and shaped like a "U" with a stem on it. It is used in tuning musical instruments and for finding pitch.

Tuning forks are made for any note on the scale—for example, A, B flat, or C above middle C. You may notice a letter and a number stamped on the tuning fork. The letter indicates the note and the number tells the frequency (number of vibrations per second). The particular note of the two tuning forks used in the *Sound* unit is not important, but it *is* important that one tuning fork is larger than the other. The larger one produces the lower pitch.

A tuning fork does not create a sound heard across the room. It produces a very localized sound that one must listen carefully to hear. Following are some tips for students' use of tuning forks in their experiments in this unit.

- To produce sound with the tuning fork, hold it by the stem and strike one prong on a soft surface—such as the heel of your hand, your knee, or the rubber sole of a shoe. (The tuning fork should not be struck on a hard surface because it can damage the tuning fork and the surface struck.)

- Strike the tuning fork firmly, letting it bounce off the surface struck so that the sound is not deadened.

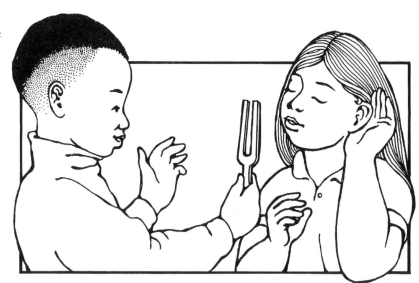

- To hear the sound of the tuning fork, hold it up to your ear after striking it. Keep your fingers off the prongs so that the sound is not deadened.

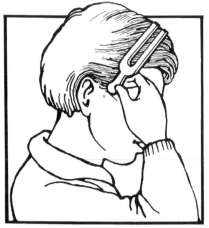

- To feel the vibrations, touch the prongs with your fingers after striking the tuning fork, or feel the vibrations in its stem.

- To amplify the sound, after striking the tuning fork put the stem on the bone in front of your ear.

4. Now ask students to write any questions they have about sound in their science notebooks. After they have done so, ask them to share their questions. Record students' responses on the chart entitled "Questions We Have about Sound," explaining that the class will be exploring these and many other questions during this unit.

    Note: You will add new ideas and questions to these charts later in the unit. For each new entry, use a different-colored marker and record the date. Students' responses on the charts will be used as a basis of comparison in the Post-Unit Assessment.

5. Ask students what they know about a tuning fork. Let them know that they will work with a partner to investigate the characteristics of tuning forks. Refer them to the tips for using tuning forks on pg. 4 in their Student Activity Books. Encourage them to find as many ways as possible to describe their observations about tuning forks and the sounds they make.

Safety Tip

Review with students the science safety rules for your classroom. In particular, you may want to remind them that putting objects in their mouths to feel vibrations is not a safe practice.

---

6. Distribute one small and one large tuning fork to each group of four students. Explain that each pair of students will have time to work with both sizes.

7. After about 5 minutes, encourage pairs of students to exchange tuning forks and continue exploring.

8. Ask students to discuss with their group the sounds they made with the tuning forks. Questions such as the following may be helpful:

    ■ How were the sounds of the tuning forks alike? How were they different?

    ■ How would you describe the sound of the small tuning fork? The large one?

    ■ What did the tuning forks feel like when they were making a sound?

Final Activities

1. To conclude the lesson, direct students' attention to the chart "Sounds We Have Heard." Ask them to think about sounds that are similar in some way and to identify a way to classify and describe these sounds. To help students get started, ask a question such as, "Which sounds do you think go together?"

2. Encourage students to share their ideas in their groups of four, comparing and discussing different ways to classify the sounds.

3. Ask students to record in their science notebooks their ideas about which sounds are similar and why they are similar.

Extensions

LANGUAGE ARTS

1. Ask students to work in pairs to think of words that produce a sound which is similar to the sounds they describe. Examples include buzz, trickle, and roar. Creating works this way is called **onomatopoeia.**

LANGUAGE ARTS

2. Ask students to make up folktales about familiar sounds. Titles for such stories might be, for example, "Where the Mosquito Got Its Buzz" and "Where the Wind Got Its Whistle."

SCIENCE

3. Take students on a "sound walk" either indoors or outdoors. Ask them to notice how many different sounds they can hear. After the walk, ask them to write and to draw pictures in their science notebooks about the sounds they heard and the source of those sounds.

MATHEMATICS

4. Challenge students to list sounds that are used to indicate time. Grandfather clocks, church bells, and schools bells come quickly to mind. Invite discussion about how the sound tells the time or how the sound indicates the amount of time elapsed.

Assessment

The main purpose of this lesson is to find out what students already know about sound so that you can assess their progress throughout the unit. Students' writing in their science notebooks and the ideas they suggest in the class brainstorming session provide an important pre-unit assessment of their knowledge of sound. In this lesson, you asked students the questions, "What are some sounds we have heard?" and "What are some ways to make sounds?" You will ask them the same questions again in the Post-Unit Assessment. By comparing responses, you will be able to assess and document both individual and class learning with respect to concepts and skills, including the following.

Concept

Sounds are produced by vibrating objects and vibrating columns of air.

- What variety and diversity of sounds do students describe for the class list?
- How do students group sounds—for example, do they group them by source, by pitch, by volume, or in other ways?

Skills

Describing the results of investigations with sound.

- How detailed are students' descriptions of the sounds made by each tuning fork?

Comparing and discussing the volume and pitch of the sounds produced.

- What comparisons do students make between sounds?

Communicating results through writing and with graphs.

- Do students date their entries?
- How complete and connected to actual results are students' written descriptions?

Performing experiments with sound.

- Do students demonstrate care when using the tuning forks?

Throughout the unit, students will be learning important skills basic to science: observing, recording, and comparing information. You can assess students' progress in these areas in two ways: (1) by observing and talking to students as they work individually and in groups, and (2) by looking at individual student products. Both approaches are important.

"Teaching *Sound*," on pgs. 5–11, includes a detailed discussion about the assessment of student learning. The specific goals and related assessments for this unit are summarized in Figure T-1, "*Sound:* Goals and Assessment Strategies," on pgs. 8–10. Keep in mind that some third-graders may not completely understand every concept listed or master every skill. As you observe your class, look for the development of these ideas and skills rather than their mastery.

LESSON 2	# How Sound Travels

Overview and Objectives

In this lesson, students explore how sound travels from place to place. Working in teams, they produce sounds with tuning forks and investigate how these sounds travel through air, wood, string, and metal. Comparing and describing the results enable students to draw conclusions and develop hypotheses about how sound travels through different materials. This sets the stage for the next five lessons, in which students investigate how vibrations produce sound.

■ Students listen to and describe sounds that are produced by tuning forks and that pass through different materials.

■ Students compare and discuss the loudness of the sounds heard.

■ Students compare and discuss what they know about how the materials vibrate.

■ Students devise and present demonstrations to support their ideas.

Background

Sound travels in the form of vibrations or waves. When sound waves hit an object, they cause the object to vibrate. Although sound can travel through all kinds of materials (solids, liquids, and gases), it travels better through some than through others.

A factor that complicates the study of sound travel is the high speed at which sound moves. It travels through air at about 330 meters (1,080 feet) per second, or about 1,190 kilometers (740 miles) per hour. Because it travels so fast, over short distances a sound often seems to occur simultaneously at the source and at the receiver. One proof that this is not happening and that sound is indeed traveling from place to place is the occurrence of an echo. Distance is needed to produce an echo, and that distance is greater than the dimensions of most classrooms. Some out-of-classroom activities that enable students to experience echoes and other examples of how sound travels are suggested in **Extensions 2–4** (pg. 25).

This lesson offers students a challenge: How can they demonstrate that sound has traveled through an object? It is hard for some students to understand that sound vibrations also travel through air. Experimenting with different materials provides experiences that lead to an understanding of these ideas, although not all students will understand them by the end of one lesson. They will continue exploring these ideas in subsequent lessons. It will be helpful for students to work together on this challenge and to discuss their observations.

Materials

For each student
1   science notebook

For every four students
1   plastic tray
1   wooden meterstick, yardstick, or similar piece of wood 1 m (39 in) long
1   piece of heavy-duty aluminum foil, 1 m (39 in) long
1   piece of heavy cotton or nylon twine, 1 m (39 in) long
1   large tuning fork
1   small tuning fork

For the class
Several sheets of newsprint
1   marker
Class chart, "Questions We Have about Sound" (from Lesson 1)

Preparation

1. Cut a sheet of aluminum foil 1 m (39 in) long for each team of four students. Fold each sheet lengthwise several times so that it looks like an aluminum-foil meterstick and is rigid.

2. Cut a 1-m (39-in) piece of heavy cotton or nylon twine for each team of four students. Different kinds of string will give different results. The black nylon fishing line included in the kit will *not* work well in this lesson.

3. If necessary, arrange to borrow wooden metersticks or yardsticks from other teachers.

4. Arrange the materials for easy collection by the teams. One suggestion is to put all the materials at a distribution center for students to collect cafeteria-style. (See Figure 2-1.)

Figure 2-1

Materials at a distribution center

Figure 2-2

Listening to sound traveling through a meterstick

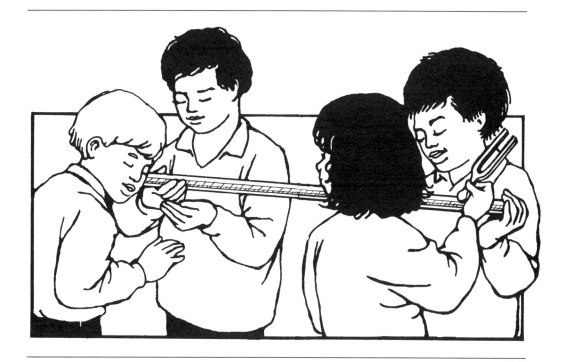

5. On a sheet of newsprint, write the title "How Sound Travels."

6. To help students hear as clearly as possible during this activity, arrange the work space so that the teams are as far apart as possible.

Procedure

1. Ask students to review how they produced sounds in Lesson 1 with the tuning forks.

2. Now challenge students to think about how sound gets from place to place. Ask them to write their ideas in their science notebooks.

3. Invite students to share some of their ideas in a class brainstorming session. Make a list of these ideas on the chart "How Sound Travels."

4. Now focus students' attention on the objects displayed at the distribution center: the wooden metersticks, the aluminum-foil metersticks, and the 1-m pieces of string. Ask them which of the objects they think sound will travel through best and why.

5. Explain that they will now investigate how sound travels. One student will hold the stem of a vibrating tuning fork near one end of the object while another student listens at the other end. (See Figure 2-2.) Let students know that when testing the string, it will work best if they wrap one end of the string around the stem of the tuning fork before striking the tuning fork; then, to listen, they can stretch the string taut between the tuning fork and their ear.

6. Challenge students to think about two questions during their investigations:

   ■ Can you hear the sound of the tuning fork through all the materials you are testing?

   ■ Which materials do you find that the sound travels through best (resulting in the loudest sound)?

7. Have students collect their materials and begin their investigations.

8. Challenge students to think of other ways to determine whether sound travels through the objects being investigated. If they do not suggest this, have them repeat the experiment, touching the end of the object with their hands rather than listening. (See Figure 2-3.) Allow time for all students to experience this investigation.

9. When they have finished testing the materials they have been given, encourage students to try other materials, such as a broom handle, window glass, their desktop, a blackboard, or a plaster wall.

Figure 2-3

Feeling vibrations of sound traveling through a meterstick

Final Activities

1. After each team has had time to investigate whether sound travels through the objects, direct students to return the materials to the distribution center.

2. Ask the teams to report what they observed to the class. Encourage students to tell what they did and what questions they now have. Add these questions to the chart from Lesson 1, "Questions We Have about Sound."

Extensions

SCIENCE

1. Have students find much larger examples of the materials they have been working with. For instance, instead of using a meterstick, they might try repeating their investigation on a long wooden table or large desk. Instead of aluminum foil, students might try using a metal chalk tray, the edge of a bulletin board, or a metal file cabinet.

SCIENCE

2. Have students create echoes to get a sense of the time required for sound to travel from place to place. Sometimes a very long, straight hallway with a closed end works well. So does a large, flat outdoor wall (such as a gymnasium wall). Ask students to clap loudly one at a time or tap two rocks together and then listen for the echo. They need to be at least 170 m (about 550 ft) from the wall to hear the echo well.

MATHEMATICS   SCIENCE

3. Ask students to watch and listen from a safe place next time there is a thunderstorm. Have them notice the time lapse between the flash of the lightning and the sound of the thunder. Ask them to write and draw pictures about their ideas of what the time lapse means.

MATHEMATICS   SCIENCE

4. If you have a large space available outside at your school, ask another adult to stand 100 m (325 ft) or more away from the class. Have the person bounce a basketball loudly or hammer a pipe. Invite students to observe whether they see the ball bounced or the pipe struck at the same time or before they hear the sound that it makes.

Making Sounds with Nails

Overview and Objectives

Students began their investigations of sound by comparing and describing the sounds produced by two different-sized tuning forks and then by exploring how sound travels from place to place. Now they focus their attention on one aspect of sound: pitch. As students begin to realize that pitch and volume are not the same, they start to develop the specific language needed to describe pitch. Exploring the sounds made by tapping three nails of different sizes introduces students to the idea that objects of different sizes can be used to produce sounds of different pitches.

- Students make predictions about the pitch that three nails of different sizes will produce when tapped with a pencil.

- Students tap the nails and compare the resulting sounds with their predictions.

- Students write descriptions of the sounds produced.

- Students identify and discuss similarities and differences between the sounds produced by tuning forks and nails.

Background

Sounds are produced by vibrating objects that make the air around them vibrate. The sounds we hear are the result of vibrations that occur within the frequency range that human hearing can detect. However, you may not always be able to see the vibrations that cause the sound. For example, the vibrations of the tuning forks could not easily be seen, but the sound was clearly heard. Other objects, such as the plucked strings of a guitar, can vibrate visibly as they produce sound.

The **frequency** of a vibration is the number of times the back-and-forth movement occurs in a second. The range of human hearing is from a frequency of about 20 vibrations per second to about 20,000 vibrations per second. Students will explore the concept of frequency through the activities in Lessons 4 and 5.

The **pitch** of a sound is determined by the frequency of the vibrations producing it. A high-pitched sound on a violin, for example, comes from a string that is producing many vibrations per second—many more than the string that produces low sounds on a cello, for example.

Pitch, however, is often confused with another characteristic of sound—volume—because both terms are commonly described by the words "high" and "low." **Volume** is measured in a unit called a **decibel.** The faintest audible sound is 0 decibels, the sound of a whisper is about 30 decibels, normal conversation is approximately 60 decibels, and the volume of a painfully loud sound created by a jet plane taking off is about 120 decibels.

As students discover in this activity, nails vibrate when struck. They produce a ringing sound similar to that of a xylophone. Larger nails produce lower-pitched sounds than smaller nails, in the same way that larger xylophone bars produce lower-pitched notes than smaller ones.

The way that a nail is held and the surface it is lying on when struck also affect how it sounds. For example, if you hold a nail in your hand while striking it, or set it on a hard surface, it will not vibrate very much. Many students probably discovered this while investigating the tuning forks in Lesson 1. Placing a nail on a convoluted sponge, however, allows it to vibrate more easily, so that the sound produced by striking it is much clearer and lasts longer.

Students need to base their predictions in this lesson on their previous experiences. Lessons 1 and 2 provided some experiences that can help them. Without such experience, they can only guess. The distinction between predicting and guessing is an important one (see **Procedure,** Step 1).

Materials

For each student

1   copy of **Record Sheet 3-A: Sounds Produced by Nails**
1   science notebook

For every two students

1   plastic tray
1   piece of convoluted foam-rubber sponge, 10×15 cm (4×6 in)
1   set of three steel nails (size 40D, 20D, and 12D)
1   unsharpened pencil (used to tap nails)

Preparation

1. Duplicate one copy of **Record Sheet 3-A: Sounds Produced by Nails** for each student.

2. Arrange the materials and record sheets at the distribution center. (See Figure 3-1).

Procedure

1. Ask students what they know about making predictions. Invite them to share their ideas with the class. The following questions may help get the discussion started:

    ■ What is the difference between a prediction and a guess? (A **prediction** is made on the basis of observation, experience, or scientific information. A **guess** is an opinion formed or a conclusion reached on the basis of little or no evidence or information.)

    ■ What are some examples of predictions? (A weather forecast, a sportscaster's prediction about which team might win a game, a student's prediction of how a scientific experiment will turn out.)

2. Review the sounds produced by the two tuning forks. How were they different and how were they similar?

3. Show the three nails to the class. Challenge students to think to themselves about the sounds the nails could make. Questions such as the following may help get them started:

    ■ When they are tapped with a pencil, will these nails all sound the same or will each one sound different from the others?

Figure 3-1

Materials ready
for distribution

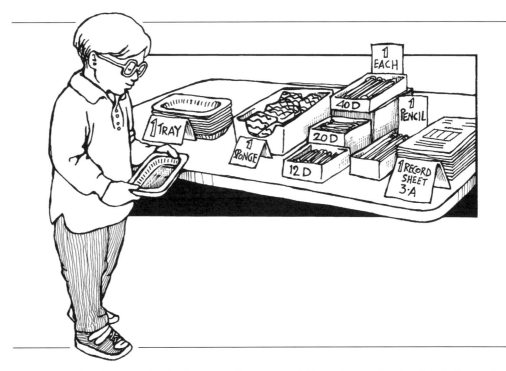

■ Why do you think the sounds will be different, or why do think they will be the same?

4. Have each pair collect their materials and two copies of **Record Sheet 3-A** from the distribution center.

5. Make sure all students understand the directions for completing Record Sheet 3-A.

6. Ask students to write their predictions about the sound that each nail will make in the column labeled "Sound Predicted" on Record Sheet 3-A. Remind them to write out reasons for their predictions.

7. Let students know that they will conduct their experiment by placing the nails on the sponge to make the sound last longer than it would on a hard surface. Ask students to test their predictions by tapping each nail with a pencil. One student should tap while the other listens (see Figure 3-2), and then they should exchange roles and repeat the activity so that all students try both activities.

Figure 3-2

Tapping a nail
and listening to
the sound

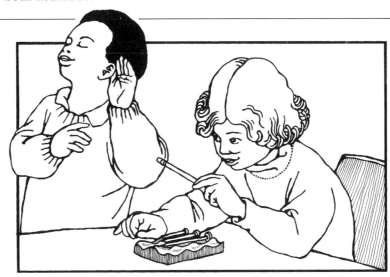

Note: The nails should be tapped quickly, but not too hard. Striking a nail too hard may cause it to bounce, stopping its vibrations or "dampening" the sound.

8. Encourage students to discuss and compare words they could use to describe the sounds they heard. They may use many different words, such as shrill, low, high, or deep.

9. After students write descriptions of the sounds produced in the column labeled "Sound Produced" on Record Sheet 3-A, have them return the materials to the distribution center.

Final Activities

1. Ask students to review their predictions and compare them with the actual sounds they heard. Then ask them to think about how they described the sounds. What words did they use? If they did use "pitch," let them know that "high" and "low" can be used to describe pitch.

2. Encourage students to describe the different pitches of the nail sounds. Which nails produced high-pitched sounds? Which nail produced the lowest-pitched sound?

3. Finally, ask students to compare the sounds made by the tuning forks with those made by the nails and to write several of their ideas in their science notebooks. If necessary, focus their thoughts by using questions about how the size of the tuning fork or nail seemed to affect the sound it made.

Extensions

SCIENCE

1. Introduce a fourth nail of a different size. Ask students to predict how the fourth nail will sound compared with the other three. Ask students to test their new prediction.

MUSIC

2. Obtain 8 to 10 nails of various sizes. Have students assemble the nails into xylophones so that they can play songs.

LANGUAGE ARTS

3. Involve students in researching the xylophone. Where did it originate? What different types of xylophones are there?

Record Sheet 3–A

Name: _____

Date: _____

Sounds Produced by Nails

Size of Nail	Sound Predicted	Sound Produced
Large		
Medium		
Small		

Reason for my predictions:

Large nail _____

Medium nail _____

Small nail _____

STC / *Sound*

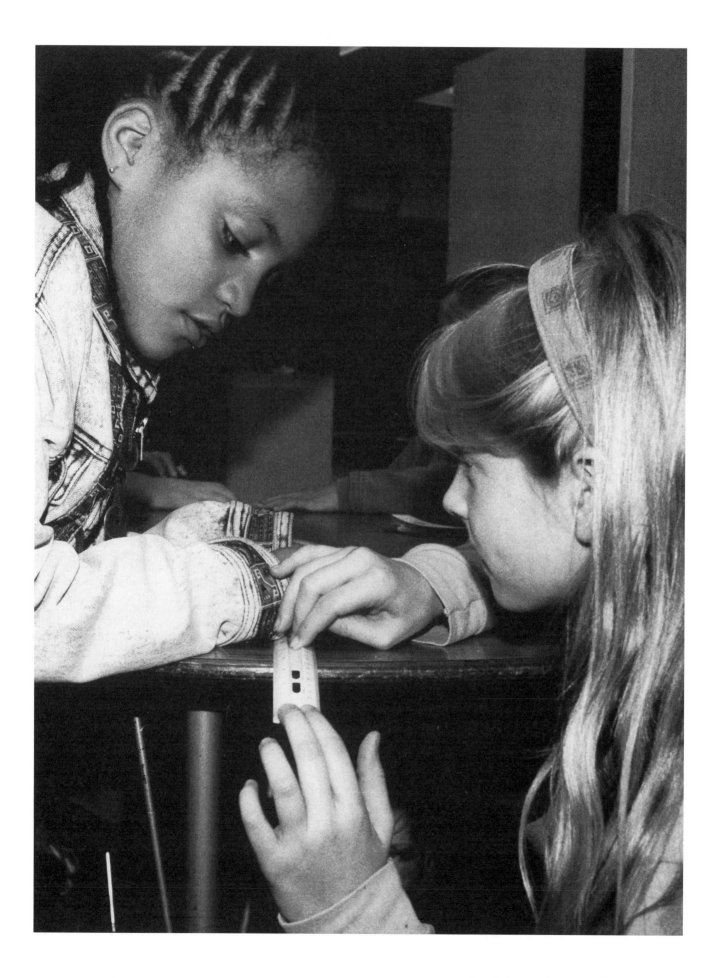

Making Sounds with Rulers

Overview and Objectives

In Lessons 1 and 3, students explored sounds made by two and then three objects that were alike except in size. In this lesson they explore the behavior of one object—a plastic ruler—that allows them to vary the length of the object that vibrates. As students investigate the range of sounds they can produce, they begin to connect the sounds they hear with the vibrations they see. They observe that as the length of the vibrating part of the ruler changes, the nature of the vibrations and the pitch of the sound produced also change. This concept is expanded and refined in the next three lessons.

- Students explore and describe sounds made by the vibrations of a ruler.

- Students observe and describe the movements of different lengths of the ruler.

- Students relate the vibrations of different lengths of the ruler to the sound produced.

- Students read to learn more about vibration and pitch.

Background

When we observe a sound-producing object, we often do not see the object vibrating. Tuning forks are an example: their vibrations are so small and of such high frequency that they are hard to see.

The activity in this lesson gives students an opportunity to actively observe vibrations that produce sound. Holding a ruler down firmly at the edge of a table with part of the ruler extending over the edge, students experiment with plucking the ruler and changing the length of the vibrating part in order to observe changes in the vibrations and the sounds produced.

Two distinctly different types of sounds can be produced by the ruler. One sound is caused by the part of the ruler vibrating in the air off the edge of the table. An additional, louder sound is that produced by the ruler slapping the table. After students have had some time for exploring, you can focus their attention on the sound produced by the part of the ruler that extends over the edge of the table (see **Procedure,** Step 6) and vibrates in the air.

Students will then have the opportunity to discover that the frequency of the ruler's vibrations is affected by the length of the part extending over the edge of the table. They will also observe that changing the length of this part causes the pitch of the sound to change: more length produces sounds with lower pitch and less length creates sounds with higher pitch.

Since no two students have had identical listening experiences, the pace at which they sort out the characteristics of sound may vary significantly. The next several lessons contain activities that provide additional opportunities for students to make sense for themselves of these phenomena. The lessons include suggestions of ways for you to observe and make note of your students' progress.

Keep in mind that a few of your students may have trouble distinguishing between sounds. Ear infections or other hearing difficulties may make it hard for some students to experience fully the phenomena they are to investigate in this lesson. (See the appendix, "Coping with Hearing Impairments," with respect to chronic hearing problems.)

Materials

For each student

1   science notebook
1   **Record Sheet 4-A: Vibrating Ruler—What I Hear and See**

For every two students

1   plastic ruler with centimeter scale, 30 cm (12 in) long
1   heavy hardback book (for example, a dictionary), about 2.5 cm (1 in) thick, from the classroom

For the class

1   sheet of newsprint
1   marker

Preparation

1.   Make one copy of **Record Sheet 4-A,** on pg. 40, for each student.

2.   Arrange for students to work in pairs.

Procedure

1.   Review with students the sounds they heard in Lessons 1 and 3 by asking them how the size of the tuning forks and nails affected the sounds they produced.

2.   Then ask students if they remember seeing the tuning forks or nails move when they were struck. Challenge students with the idea that they will want to keep both their eyes and ears open as they test the sound-making device in today's lesson.

3.   Show students a plastic ruler and ask them to think about how the ruler could produce sounds.

4.   Have each pair of students pick up one ruler, one book, and two copies of **Record Sheet 4-A** from the distribution center.

5.   Encourage students to explore making sounds with the ruler. Then suggest that they extend one end of the ruler over the edge of the table, pluck it, and listen. Which sounds come from the ruler hitting the table? Which are produced by the ruler making the air vibrate?

6.   Focus students' attention on the sounds produced by the ruler making the air vibrate. If necessary, show them how to hold the ruler down firmly with a book so they are not distracted by the noise of the ruler hitting the table. (See Figure 4-1.)

7.   Ask students to recall their experiments in Lessons 1 and 3, and then to think about whether the ruler might make sounds of high or low pitch when

Figure 4-1

Plucking the ruler and seeing its vibrations

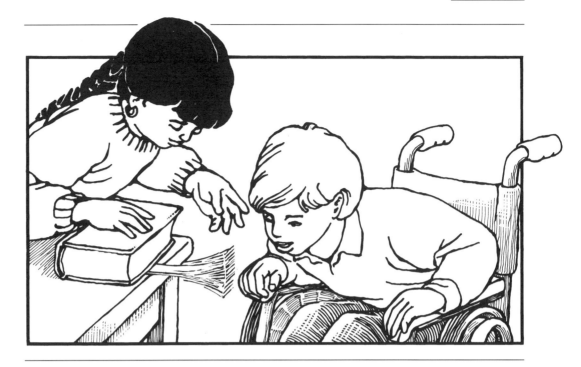

a long piece of it extends over the edge of the table. Why do they think so? Have students write their predictions about the sound produced by a long, medium, and short piece of the ruler on Record Sheet 4-A, in the column labeled "Predictions and Reasons," under the heading "What I Hear."

Note: Remind students that in order to measure and read the number of centimeters, they will want to have the "zero centimeter" end of the ruler extending over the edge, not hidden under the book. Also remind them to include the unit of measure—cm—with the number in recording their data.

8. Now ask students to make predictions about how they think the ruler will vibrate when a long, medium, and short piece extends over the edge of the table. They should make their predictions in the column labeled "Predictions and Reasons," under the heading "What I See" on **Record Sheet 4-A.**

9. Ask students to work with their partners to investigate the sounds produced by plucking different lengths of the ruler. Have them record what they see and hear. Have them write notes in their science notebooks about what they see and hear.

10. After students finish exploring the behavior of various lengths of the vibrating ruler, have them return their materials to the distribution center.

11. Ask students to use the information they have collected to complete Record Sheet 4-A. An example of a completed record sheet is shown in Figure 4-2.

Final Activities

1. Ask students to share what they discovered as they listened to different pitches and saw the rulers vibrating. Questions such as the following may help start the discussion:

   ■ What did you hear when you compared the sound produced by a long piece of the ruler with the sound of a short piece?

   ■ What did you observe when you compared the vibrations of a long piece and a short piece of the ruler?

Figure 4-2

Example of completed record sheet

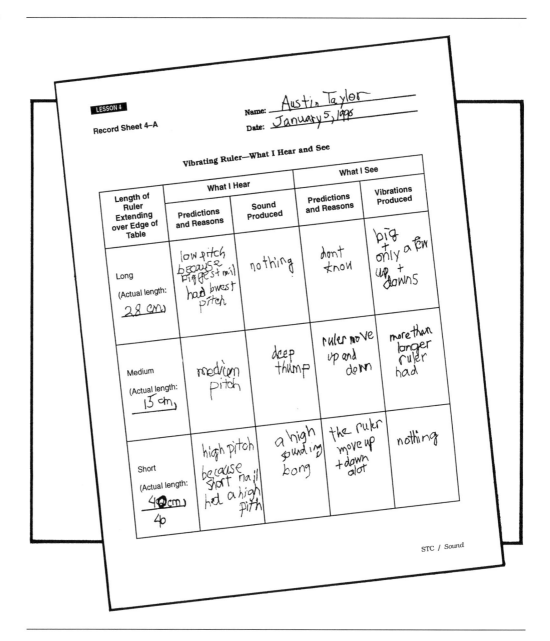

2. Introduce "The Elephant's Rumble," on pgs. 38–39 of the Teacher's Guide and pgs. 16–17 of the Student Activity Book, by asking students to make a list of animals and the sounds they make. Then challenge them to brainstorm ways they think animals produce these sounds.

Note: The reading selection "The Elephant's Rumble" and Extension 3 in this lesson refer to a book entitled *Elephants Calling*. The Bibliography in this unit provides a full citation and an annotation for this and other books mentioned in the unit.

Extensions

> **SCIENCE**

1. Ask students to find objects other than rulers that can be placed over the edge of the table and plucked to make sounds of different pitches. Challenge students to match the pitches of two different vibrating objects.

SOCIAL STUDIES

2. Invite a policeman or policewoman to bring dog whistles and a dog to the classroom. Ask the visitor to share and discuss the "silent whistle" with students.

LANGUAGE ARTS

3. Read *Elephants Calling,* by Katharine Payne, to the class.

SCIENCE

4. Challenge students to find out more about how different animals hear and about the complex communication systems that some animals use.

Assessment

This is the first in a series of three lessons containing activities that involve students in changing the frequency and pitch of sounds. Students' work during these lessons will be useful when assessing their progress. As you read notebook entries, examine record sheets, and listen to discussions during these three lessons, look for the following.

Concepts

■ Do students understand that sound is produced by vibrations?

■ How do students distinguish between pitch and volume?

■ Do students recognize the effect that changing the length of the ruler has on the pitch?

Skills

■ What words do students use to describe the different pitches produced by an object?

■ Do students make predictions that include reasons based on previous experiences?

■ Do students demonstrate progress in organizing and recording their results?

■ Do students demonstrate increased application of previous observations to new experiences?

■ Do students show growth in responsibility for collecting and returning their own science materials?

■ Are students using materials appropriately?

■ How do students see connections between the information in the reading selection and their own investigations?

**Reading
Selection**

The Elephant's Rumble

Sit quietly for a moment and listen to the sounds around you. What do you hear? Do you hear sounds made by people? Do you hear sounds made by machines? Do you hear any sounds made by animals—for example, the barking of dogs? What other sounds have you heard animals make? Have you heard the roar of a lion, the moo of a cow, the meow of a cat, the hoot of an owl, or the squeak of a hamster?

One sound that probably would not be on your list is the "elephant's rumble." You probably could not hear it even if you were standing right in the elephant house at the zoo. If an elephant made this sound, your human ears might hear a soft rumbling or you might hear nothing at all. Elephants, however, would hear this sound very clearly.

Elephants also make sounds that human ears *can* hear. They bellow. They make trumpeting sounds.

Why, then, can't we hear their rumble? The rumble has a very low pitch. It is lower than the lowest pitch human ears can hear. ("Low" as it is used here does not mean "quiet." A low-pitched sound is a deep sound. An example would be the sound made by the horn of a tugboat.) When the elephant vibrates the air inside its trunk to make the rumbling sound, the pitch of the sound is *very, very* low. A special name is given to this kind of sound. It is **infrasound.** The word means "below sound."

No one knew about the elephant's rumble until quite recently. In the 1980s, a scientist named Katharine Payne discovered this sound and began to study it. Later, she wrote a book for young people about elephants and their rumble. In the book, *Elephants Calling,* she explains that

infrasound can travel much farther than most sounds that human ears can hear. Katharine Payne's studies showed that elephants use infrasound to send messages to other elephants that are miles away. She used special tape recorders to record these sounds that human ears cannot hear.

What kinds of messages are elephants sending each other over such long distances? According to Katharine Payne, they are giving and receiving important information. For example, their messages can help other elephants find the food and water they need.

The low rumbles of elephants can make the air vibrate, or throb, almost like the rumbling of distant thunder. If you can visit elephants at the zoo, notice whether you feel the air throbbing. If you do, maybe it is because the elephants are calling to each other with infrasound.

If infrasound is so *low* human ears cannot hear it, can you guess what ultrasound is? **Ultrasound** is at a *higher* pitch than what human ears can hear. The dog is one animal that can hear some high-pitched sounds which we cannot. In fact, there is a special kind of whistle made for dogs. If you blew one of these dog whistles, you would not hear a thing, but your dog would. So just as you would be considerate of human ears when blowing a whistle, remember to be considerate of dogs' ears when blowing a dog whistle!

Record Sheet 4–A

Name: _____

Date: _____

Vibrating Ruler—What I Hear and See

Length of Ruler Extending over Edge of Table	What I Hear		What I See	
	Predictions and Reasons	**Sound Produced**	**Predictions and Reasons**	**Vibrations Produced**
Long (Actual length: _____)				
Medium (Actual length: _____)				
Short (Actual length: _____)				

Exploring Pitch

Overview and Objectives

Building on students' previous investigations with a ruler, this lesson allows them to focus on the frequency of the vibrations as they continue exploring the connection between vibrations and pitch. By closely observing the ruler's vibrations as they listen to different sounds, students gain a deeper understanding of the relationship of the frequency of the vibrations, the length of the ruler that is vibrating, and the pitch of the resulting sound. Comparing sounds made by following a pattern of ruler lengths enables students to begin differentiating and quantifying a range of pitches.

- Students observe, describe, and compare the frequencies produced by different lengths of a vibrating ruler.

- Students test how to make the pitch of the sound higher or lower.

- Students construct a chart to relate what they have learned about length, frequency, and pitch.

- Students review and summarize their data and ideas about the sounds they have made.

Background

The range of vibrations that we can both see and hear is very small. Human eyes tend to perceive only a blur of motion when objects vibrate more frequently than about 60 times per second. At this and higher frequencies, human sight cannot see the individual back-and-forth movements of the vibrating object. On the other hand, human ears cannot hear sound produced by vibrations that have a frequency of less than 20 times per second. The vibrating ruler is useful in this lesson because it is capable of vibrating within this range of frequencies that we can both see and hear, between 20 and 60 times per second.

Interpreting observations of the vibrating ruler is challenging. When the ruler is vibrating at a rate low enough to enable students to count the back-and-forth motions, it probably will not produce an audible pitch. When the length of the vibrating ruler is made short enough for the pitch of the sound to become audible, students will not be able to actually count the vibrations.

Students can, however, observe and feel the vibrations of the ruler that is producing the sound. From this, they can *infer* that as the vibrating part of the ruler becomes shorter, the frequency of the vibrations increases. Although they will not be able to actually count the vibrations, they will be able to observe and feel a difference in the vibrations as they change the length of the vibrating ruler to produce sounds of different pitches.

Materials

For each student

1   science notebook

1   **Record Sheet 5-A: Vibrating Rulers—Hearing and Seeing Patterns**

For every two students

2   plastic rulers with centimeter scale, 30 cm (12 in) long

1   heavy hardback book (for example, a dictionary), about 2.5 cm (1 in) thick, from the classroom

Preparation

Make one copy of **Record Sheet 5-A: Vibrating Rulers—Hearing and Seeing Patterns,** on pg. 47, for each student.

Procedure

1. Ask students to recall and describe the different sounds that they made with a ruler in Lesson 4. What did they do to produce sounds of different pitches?

2. Distribute one ruler and one heavy book to each pair of students. Challenge them to investigate the sounds produced by lengths of the ruler that correspond to a "number pattern" in centimeters (cm): for example, 10 cm, 15 cm, 20 cm, and 25 cm—or 8 cm, 12 cm, 16 cm, and 20 cm.

3. Have students continue exploring until they find four lengths that allow them to hear at least four different pitches distinctly.

4. Challenge the pairs to decide on a way to describe these four pitches. Series of designations they might choose, for example, could be: "Highest/high/low/ lowest," or "High/medium-high/medium-low/low."

5. Invite the pairs of students to get a second ruler. As one student holds the two rulers at different lengths firmly under the book and plucks them, the partner can listen and observe. Then the partners can switch roles and repeat the activity, as shown in Figures 5-1(a) and (b). Can they hear *and* see a difference when the rulers are at different lengths?

Figure 5-1(a)
Seeing rulers vibrate

Figure 5-1(b)
Hearing rulers vibrate

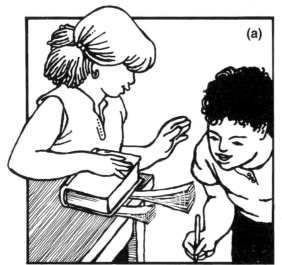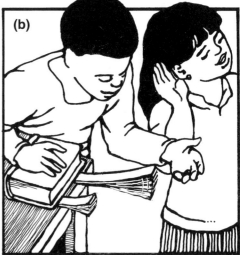

Figure 5-2

Four vibrating rulers

6. After pairs of students have explored with two rulers, move them into groups of four. Challenge them to arrange the four rulers in sequence—for example, 10 cm, 15 cm, 20 cm, 25 cm—and to test this pattern by plucking the four rulers quickly, one after the other, in both ascending and descending order. Students may notice a crude "scale." (See Figure 5-2.)

7. Have students return their materials to the distribution center.

8. Distribute **Record Sheet 5-A** and have students record what they observed. (See Figure 5-3 for an example of a completed record sheet.)

Final Activities

1. Ask students to compare their results with those of other groups, identifying how the vibrations they saw and the sounds they heard were related.

2. To end the lesson, have students review all the data they have gathered in the unit so far—record sheets and notebooks entries. Ask them to write several sentences in their science notebooks to summarize what they now know about sound.

Extensions

SCIENCE

1. Ask students to pair up and play a guessing game with their partners. Have one student pluck the ruler while the other student looks the other way and predicts the length of the ruler producing the pitch. Then students can switch roles.

Figure 5-3

Example of completed record sheet

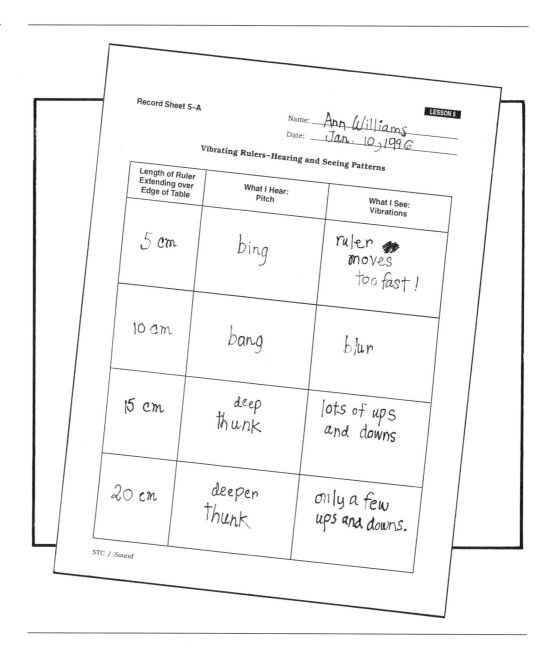

Record Sheet 5-A

Name: *Ann Williams*

Date: *Jan. 10, 1996*

Vibrating Rulers–Hearing and Seeing Patterns

Length of Ruler Extending over Edge of Table	What I Hear: Pitch	What I See: Vibrations
5 cm	bing	ruler moves too fast!
10 cm	bang	blur
15 cm	deep thunk	lots of ups and downs
20 cm	deeper thunk	only a few ups and downs.

STC / *Sound*

MUSIC

2. Ask students to work in small teams to try to play a tune with ruler lengths. One example ("Twinkle, Twinkle, Little Star") is shown below. You may want to let students make up their own songs, or assign different ruler lengths to groups of students so that the entire class can participate.

   Song: 14 14 10 10 9 9 10 11 11 12 12 13 13 14 (cm)

LANGUAGE ARTS

3. Have students discuss how descriptions of sound—such as "creaking stairs" or "howling wind"—can create mood. Then ask them to write stories using descriptive sound phrases.

Record Sheet 5–A

Name: _____

Date: _____

Vibrating Rulers—Hearing and Seeing Patterns

Length of Ruler Extending over Edge of Table	What I Hear: Pitch	What I See: Vibrations

Vibrations We Can't See

Overview and Objectives

In previous lessons, students observed vibrations when rulers produced sound. In this lesson, they are introduced to sounds produced without visible vibrations by experimenting with a slide whistle. Through their observations and discussions, students begin to consider that sounds can be produced by the vibration of air. The graph resulting from this investigation provides students with an example of the relationship between the length of the column of vibrating air and pitch. Reading about how this relationship is used in making musical instruments sets the stage for Lesson 7, in which students apply their knowledge to designing and building their own wind instruments.

- Students make predictions about length and the pitch of a whistle.

- Students investigate how to vary the pitch produced by a slide whistle.

- Students construct a graph to record their observations.

- Students read about how the relationship between air-column length and pitch is applied in making several other wind instruments.

Background

Sound is not always produced by objects that vibrate visibly like the rulers that students explored in previous lessons. For example, in some musical instruments—such as the slide whistle used in this lesson—sound is produced by a vibrating column of air. Although the air within the whistle is vibrating, those vibrations cannot be observed directly.

Instead of blowing into the slide whistle in these investigations, students will use a squeeze bulb to blow air through the tube of the whistle. This provides an effective way to generate sound without spreading germs or creating excessively loud sounds. Figure 6-1 shows the slide whistle provided in the kit.

Using this whistle, students can vary the pitch produced by changing the length of the vibrating column of air inside the tube. The clear plastic tube lets students see and measure the length of the column of air.

Students can also change the whistle's pitch by forcing more or less air through it. Forcing a small amount of air through the whistle with the squeeze bulb will produce low-pitched sounds. But if a student pounds on the squeeze bulb with a fist, the whistle will produce shrill, very high pitched sounds, called **overtones.** Both the lower-pitched sounds and these high overtones can be varied by using the slide to change the length of the column of air.

Figure 6-1

A slide whistle

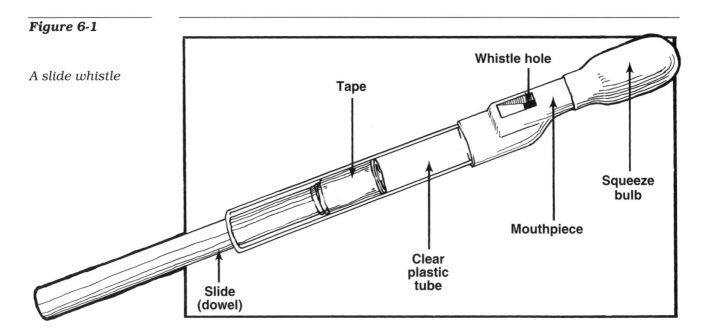

The reading selection "Wind Instruments around the World" expands on the theme of vibrating columns of air, again focusing students' attention on the relationship between pitch and the length of the column of air.

Materials

For each student
1   science notebook
1   copy of **Record Sheet 6-A: Whistle Sounds**

For every two students
1   plastic tray
1   whistle mouthpiece
1   plastic tube, 15-mm (⅝-in) diameter, 10.5 cm (4¼ in) long
1   squeeze bulb
1   wooden dowel, 14-mm (%₆-in) diameter, 15 cm (6 in) long
1   plastic ruler with centimeter scale, 30 cm (12 in) long

For the class
1   assembled slide whistle
3   rolls of masking tape

Preparation

1. See **Student Instructions for Assembling a Slide Whistle,** on pg. 53 of the Teacher's Guide and pg. 25 of the Student Activity Book. Put together a slide whistle so that you can show the class how it works.

2. Duplicate one copy of **Record Sheet 6-A: Whistle Sounds,** on pg. 56, for each student.

Procedure

1. Ask students to think about how a whistle works. Encourage them to exchange ideas in small groups before you begin a class discussion. Questions like the following might help them focus:

   ■ Describe a whistle you have seen or used.

   ■ How do you think a whistle produces sounds?

   ■ What would you need to make a whistle?

   ■ What might you do to change the pitch of the sound that a whistle makes?

2. Show students the slide whistle you assembled. Now ask them to write a prediction in their science notebooks about the pitch of the whistle when the slide is all the way in and another prediction about the pitch when the slide is only halfway in. Have them draw the whistle with each of their predictions.

3. Distribute the materials for making slide whistles to each pair of students. Review the **Student Instructions for Assembling a Slide Whistle,** on pg. 53 of this guide and pg. 25 of the Student Activity Book.

Safety Tip

To prevent the spread of germs, remind students not to blow into the slide whistles but to use the squeeze bulbs to produce sounds.

---

4. Allow time for students, working in pairs, to explore producing sounds with the whistle. Facilitate this exploration with questions such as, "What happens when you move the slide?"

5. When students find the position of the slide that produces the sound with the lowest pitch, ask them to measure the distance from the slide to the bottom of the whistle hole. They should record this information on the chart, labeled "Recording Our Observations," at the top of **Record Sheet 6-A.** (Note that the graph at the bottom of the record sheet has no entries less than 3 cm, because the distance from the whistle hole to the bottom of the mouthpiece is about 3 cm.)

Figure 6-2

*Measuring a
slide whistle*

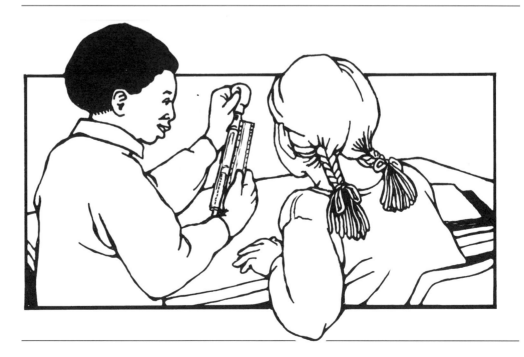

6. Have students repeat Step 5, this time looking for the position that produces the sound with the highest pitch.

7. Invite students to continue experimenting with their whistles, measuring the distance from the slide to the whistle hole and describing the pitches produced.

8. Have students return their whistles to the distribution center.

Final Activities

1. Ask students to use the information they recorded on their charts to construct the graph, labeled "Graphing Our Observations," at the bottom of **Record Sheet 6-A.** (See Figure 6-3.)

2. Encourage students to look at their classmates' graphs and to compare and discuss their results.

3. Ask students to read "Wind Instruments around the World," on pgs. 54–55 of the Teacher's Guide and pgs. 26–27 of the Student Activity Book.

Figure 6-3

Example of completed graph from Record Sheet 6-A

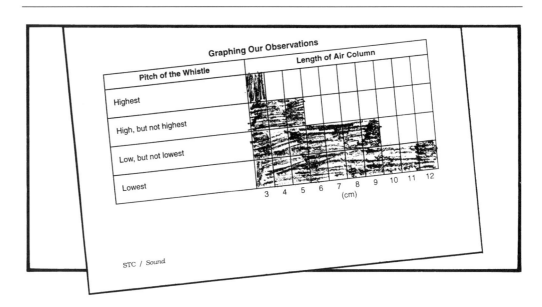

Extensions

> **SCIENCE**

1. Invite students to bring in whistles and other musical toys from home. Establish a learning center where they can explore similarities and differences in the sounds produced.

> **MUSIC**

2. Listen to a recording of wind instruments. Invite students to share what they know about the various instruments.

Student Instructions for Assembling a Slide Whistle

1. Attach the rubber squeeze bulb to the end of the whistle mouthpiece.

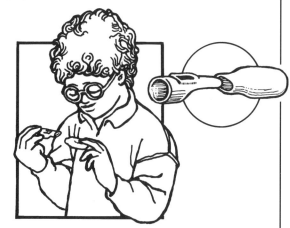

2. Attach the whistle mouthpiece to the plastic tube.

3. To make the slide, wrap masking tape around one end of the dowel so it fits snugly inside the tube but still slides easily.

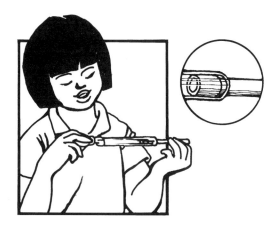

4. Test your slide whistle by squeezing the bulb. What happens when you change the position of the slide?

Reading Selection

Wind Instruments around the World

Do you know that people all over the world have made musical instruments out of simple things for thousands of years? They have invented many instruments that use a vibrating column of air to produce sounds. They have made these instruments out of things they found lying around or growing nearby, such as bamboo, horns from cows and other animals, seashells, and many other things.

People in many different countries have made a simple instrument called the "panpipe." Today panpipes are often played in South American countries. Panpipes are made of a set of tubes joined together. The tubes can be made of wood, bamboo, or clay.

To make music, the panpipe player blows across the top of the tubes, just as you might blow across the top of a bottle to make a sound. This makes the air in the tubes vibrate. The air vibrating in the shortest tube has the highest pitch. The air vibrating in the longer tubes produces lower pitches.

Playing a panpipe

Other musical instruments besides the panpipe have pipes of different lengths. One of them uses a bag of air! The bag is often made of animal skin such as goatskin. Can you guess what the instrument is? It is a bagpipe.

Bagpipes are played in many parts of the world. One well-known kind of bagpipe is played in Scotland. Other types of bagpipes are played in Africa, Asia, and other countries in Europe besides Scotland.

To play a Scottish bagpipe, the piper blows air into the bag and then forces the air out of the bag through three pipes. If you have ever heard a bagpipe played, you probably remember its special sound.

Playing a Scottish bagpipe

Herders in the mountains of Switzerland make alphorns of wood. When a Swiss alphorn is played, it echoes through the mountains. If you have not heard the alphorn played, perhaps you can guess what kind of sounds it makes. As the picture shows, it is a very long instrument.

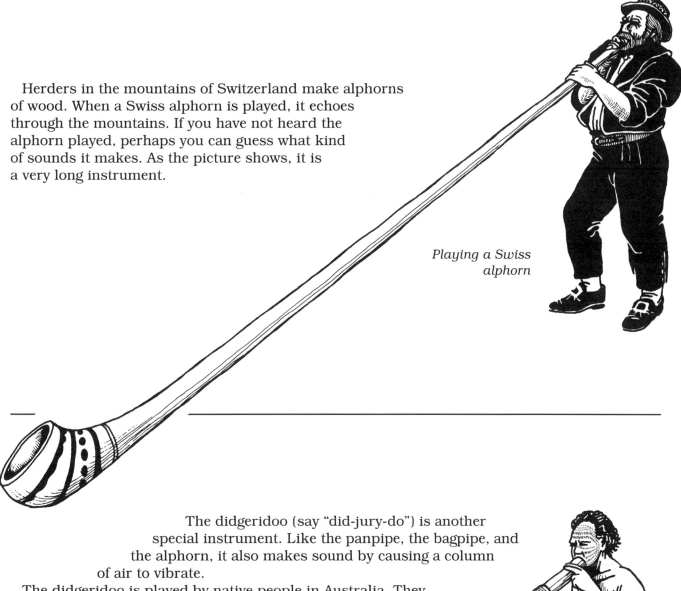

Playing a Swiss alphorn

The didgeridoo (say "did-jury-do") is another special instrument. Like the panpipe, the bagpipe, and the alphorn, it also makes sound by causing a column of air to vibrate.

The didgeridoo is played by native people in Australia. They make this instrument with the help of insects! This is what they do. They bury a long branch from the eucalyptus (say "you-ca-lip-tus") tree in the ground. Insects called termites find the branch under the ground and eat the inside of it. The hollow tube is then dug up, painted, and played. The didgeridoo shown in the picture is quite long. What kind of sound do you think it makes?

Playing a didgeridoo

The panpipe, bagpipe, alphorn, and didgeridoo are only four examples of wind instruments. There are hundreds of others. Can you name any?

Record Sheet 6–A

Name: _____

Date: _____

Whistle Sounds

Recording Our Observations

Pitch of the Whistle	Length of Air Column
Highest	
High, but not highest	
Low, but not lowest	
Lowest	

Graphing Our Observations

Pitch of the Whistle	Length of Air Column									
Highest										
High, but not highest										
Low, but not lowest										
Lowest										
	3	4	5	6	7	8	9	10	11	12

(cm)

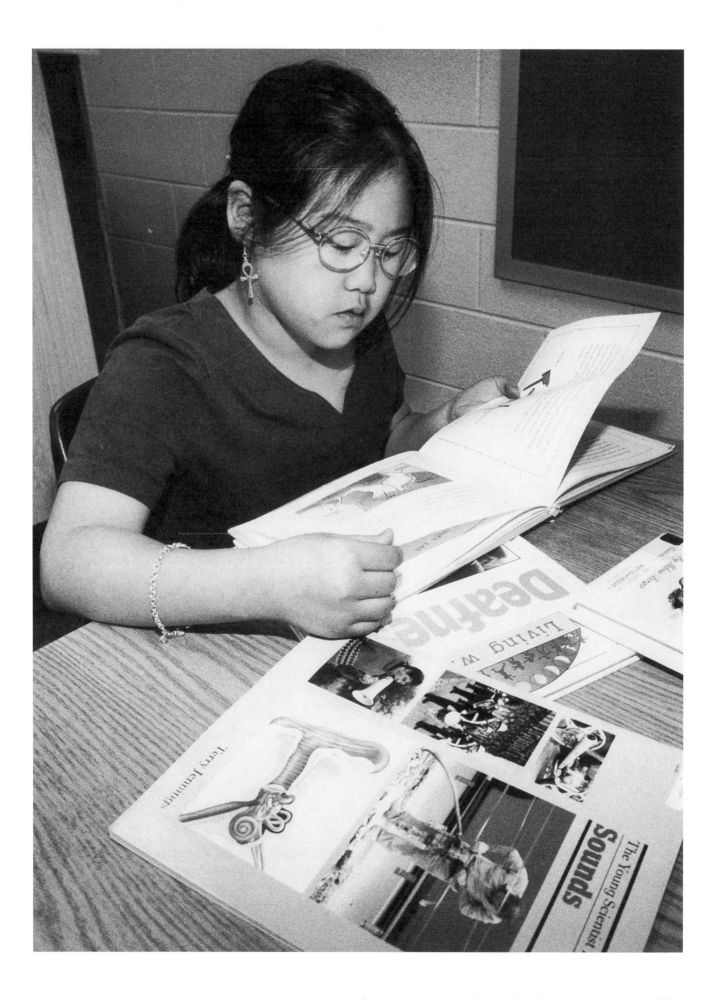

Designing a Reed Instrument

Overview and Objectives

In Lesson 6, students had the opportunity to investigate how sounds can be produced by a vibrating column of air when they constructed a slide whistle. They also did experiments to see how the pitch of the sounds produced by the whistle can be varied. In Lesson 7, an embedded assessment, students apply what they have learned about sounds produced by vibrating columns of air as they design another type of wind instrument—one that uses a vibrating reed. This lesson will give teachers an opportunity to see if students can apply to the design and construction of their own reed instrument what they have learned about the relationship between the length of a vibrating air column and the pitch of the sound that is produced.

- Students design and construct a reed instrument.

- Students describe and demonstrate the instruments they have made.

- Students explain how they have designed their instruments to produce sounds of different pitch.

- Students share ideas and questions they have about the sounds produced by different kinds of wind instruments.

Background

In Lesson 6, students experimented with the sounds produced by a slide whistle—a wind instrument that uses a whistle to set up vibrations in a column of air. Other musical instruments that operate on the same principle as the slide whistle include flutes, recorders, organ pipes, and many folk instruments, such as panpipes, tin flutes, and ocarinas.

Students will also be aware that there are other kinds of wind instruments that use different methods of creating vibrations in a column of air. **Brass instruments** are one other important group of wind instruments. Brass instruments have a cup-shaped mouthpiece, which enables a musician to produce sound vibrations by blowing a stream of air through tightly compressed lips. Brass wind instruments include trumpets and cornets, trombones, French horns, and tubas.

Another important group of wind instruments is reed instruments, which use a vibrating reed to create sound vibrations in the air column. The large family of reed instruments includes two subgroups, based on the construction of the reed. **Single-reed instruments** include clarinets and saxophones, which have a mouthpiece containing a single thin piece of vibrating wood. **Double-reed instruments,** such as oboes, English horns, and bassoons, have a mouthpiece that is constructed of two reeds pressed together. This is the type of reed instrument that students will be constructing in this lesson.

This lesson will provide an opportunity for students to apply what they have learned thus far about sound to the construction of a reed instrument of their own design. The design and construction work can be started at school but continued at home.

Students will want to be able to share what they have done. If they are encouraged to make presentations in groups of four, they will benefit from the opportunity to discuss their ideas with one another, reflect on their common experiences, and develop a well-thought-out presentation for the class.

For the teacher, these student presentations will provide an opportunity to assess what students are thinking and how far their conceptual understanding of sound has progressed. The most successful demonstrations will occur when students feel safe about taking the risk of sharing what they really think. If they can speak freely, without worrying about "getting the right answer," these presentations will provide an effective tool for assessing student progress.

Materials

For each student
1 science notebook
6 plastic "Jumbo" drinking straws
6 plastic "Super-Jumbo" drinking straws
1 copy of blackline master, **Ideas for Straw Reed Instruments**

For every four students
1 hole punch
1 pair of scissors

Preparation

1. Arrange the materials for students to collect at the distribution center.

2. Duplicate a copy of the blackline master **Ideas for Straw Reed Instruments** for each student.

3. Make a straw reed (see **Student Instructions for Making Straw Reed Instruments,** on pgs. 63–64 of the Teacher's Guide and pgs. 31–32 of the Student Activity Book) and experiment with making sounds. You can experiment with different lengths of reeds, but generally cutting a wedge about 1 cm (½ in) long works well.

   Note: You and your students may have to practice before you succeed in making a sound with the straw reed. You may find it helpful to flatten the reed by pulling it between your thumbnail and forefinger before blowing through it (see the Student Instructions). Then, to play the straw reed instrument, try closing your lips around the straw, pressing gently on the "reed" (the cut end), partially closing it as you blow. You might also try slightly squeezing the straw with your fingers just in front of your lips as you blow. Take rests between breaths and blow gently to avoid becoming light-headed. You will find that you do not have to blow very hard to make a sound.

Procedure

1. Review the **Student Instructions for Making Straw Reed Instruments,** on pgs. 63–64 of this guide and pgs. 31–32 of the Student Activity Book. Demonstrate how to construct a straw reed from one of the thinner ("Jumbo") plastic straws.

2. Invite students to collect their materials from the distribution center. Encourage students to construct their own straw reeds.

3. You will probably need to circulate around the class to help individual students begin to produce a sound successfully.

Management Tip: Have a box of tissues handy when students experiment with blowing through the straws, since saliva often gets blown through the straws together with air.

4. Challenge students to design a drinking straw reed instrument that will produce at least four different pitches.

5. Distribute the blackline master **Ideas for Straw Reed Instruments.** If students find it difficult getting started, ask them what might happen if they tried the following:

   ■ Cut the straws to different lengths.

   ■ Combine several straws into a long one. (This can be done without tape, by flaring the end of one straw with the sharpened end of a pencil, so that a second straw can be inserted inside the flared end. See the Student Instructions for Making Straw Reed Instruments.)

   ■ Use the hole punch to create a series of holes along the side of the straw (see the Student Instructions) and then use their fingers to cover various combinations of holes as they blow the straw reed.

   ■ Insert a straw with a smaller diameter into a straw with a larger diameter to create a trombonelike instrument (see the Student Instructions).

6. Allow ample time for students to create their inventions and experiment with them.

7. Invite students to draw and describe their instruments in their science notebooks. Remind them to be prepared to describe the sounds produced and to answer questions from their classmates.

Final Activities

1. Have students in their groups of four share what they have learned.

2. Invite the groups to discuss how they want to demonstrate their results to the class. For example, they might want to discuss and demonstrate what the group had learned about sound that influenced the design of their straw reed instruments. Or they might want to play a few bars of a familiar tune such as "Mary Had a Little Lamb" or "Jingle Bells" to demonstrate the different pitches their instruments make.

3. Have the groups take turns demonstrating and discussing their instruments.

4. Allow students time to ask each other questions.

Extensions

LANGUAGE ARTS

1. Presentations in this lesson provide an opportunity to invite parents to attend and observe what students are learning. You may want to give your students more time to prepare their presentations if visitors will be attending.

LANGUAGE ARTS

2. Challenge students to prepare sound effects for a radio play. Make an audio- or videotape of the play so that students can review their performances.

Assessment

The activities in this lesson offer you an opportunity to assess how your students' thinking has progressed with respect to the following concepts and skills.

Concepts

■ Do students understand that sound can be produced by vibrating columns of air?

■ Does the design of the students' reed instruments demonstrate an understanding that pitch is related to the length of the air column?

Skills

■ Do students apply previously learned concepts and skills in designing a their own wind instruments?

■ Do they experiment with different designs?

■ Do they compare and discuss the pitch of the sounds produced?

■ Do they communicate the results of their investigations through writing and with drawings?

■ Are students able to share the results of their investigations with sound?

Student Instructions for Making Straw Reed Instruments

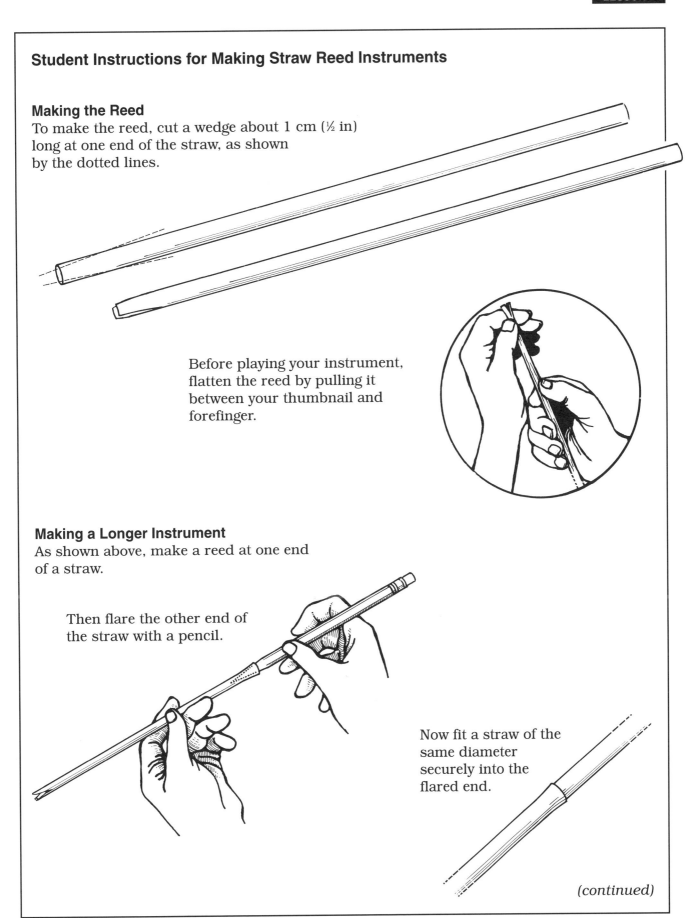

Making the Reed

To make the reed, cut a wedge about 1 cm (½ in) long at one end of the straw, as shown by the dotted lines.

Before playing your instrument, flatten the reed by pulling it between your thumbnail and forefinger.

Making a Longer Instrument

As shown above, make a reed at one end of a straw.

Then flare the other end of the straw with a pencil.

Now fit a straw of the same diameter securely into the flared end.

(continued)

Making an Instrument with Finger Holes
As shown before, make a reed at one end
of a straw.

Now punch holes in the side of the straw using a hole punch.
(It will help if you make the holes so that they are at the top
of the instrument when you play it.)

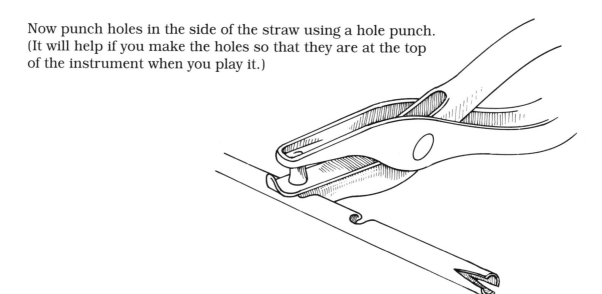

Making a Slide Instrument
Take two straws—one with smaller
diameter and one with larger
diameter.

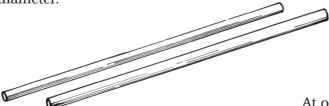

At one end of the straw with the smaller
diameter, make a reed as shown before.

Insert the other end of the straw with the smaller diameter into
the straw with the larger diameter.

Ideas for Straw Reed Instruments

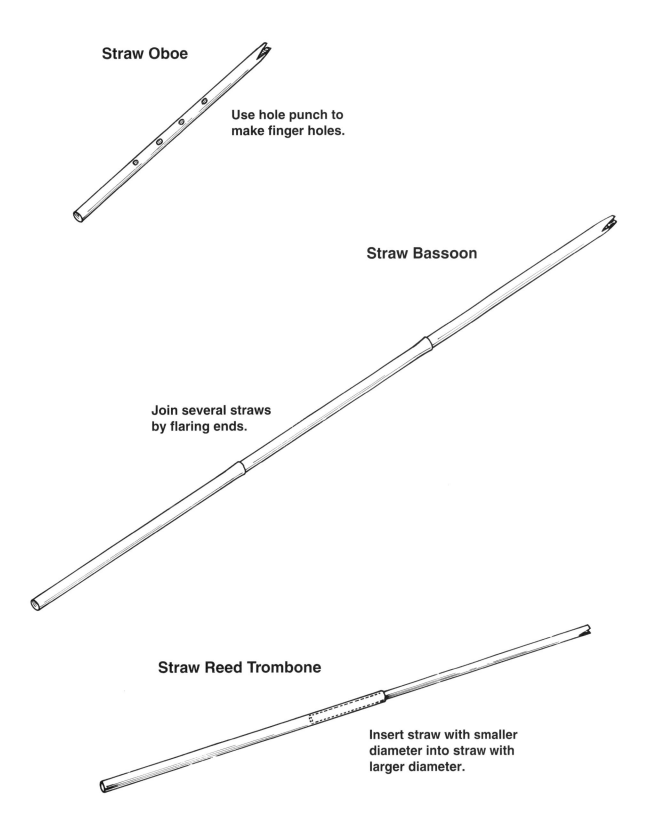

Straw Oboe

Use hole punch to make finger holes.

Straw Bassoon

Join several straws by flaring ends.

Straw Reed Trombone

Insert straw with smaller diameter into straw with larger diameter.

Making a Model Eardrum

Overview and Objectives

So far in this unit, students have observed and demonstrated that sounds are caused by vibrations. This lesson helps students discover a related aspect of sound: not only do vibrations cause sound, but sound vibrations in the air in turn can cause objects they strike to vibrate. This discovery provides students with the knowledge they need to investigate the workings of the human ear as they observe vibrations of a model eardrum. From their experiments, students can draw conclusions about how distance affects the intensity of the vibrations received by the ear. Discussions of their investigations and of a reading selection allow students to reflect on their observations and to increase their understanding of hearing and the human ear.

- Students construct a model of the eardrum.

- Students produce vibrations in the membrane of the model eardrum.

- Students describe and discuss the vibrations observed.

- Students investigate how distance affects the vibrations received by the model eardrum.

- Students read to learn more about the human eardrum and hearing.

Background

As discussed in Lesson 2, sound travels in waves. When sound waves travelling through air strike an object, the air vibrations can make the object vibrate. The sounds produced by thunder, fireworks, or a jackhammer can result in vibrations that have great energy. At times we can actually feel the vibrations from these loud sounds.

Most sounds are less intense than these loud sounds, and when the sound vibrations from softer sounds reach other objects, those vibrations cannot be felt. Our eardrums are an exception; the eardrum is a thin, flexible tissue that vibrates even when very soft sounds strike it. In this lesson, students construct a model eardrum from a piece of thin rubber stretched over a plastic cup to investigate how the eardrum can act as a detector of sound vibrations.

Although students will be focusing on one important part of the human ear, the eardrum, they may be interested in a simple description of how that part works together with the other parts of the ear to allow them to hear. The ear consists of three main parts: the outer, middle, and inner ear. The outer ear, which includes the visible part, collects sounds. If students cup a hand behind one ear and turn toward the source of some sound, they may notice how much louder the sound seems. The hand is acting as an extension of the outer ear as it collects sound.

The outer ear is also like a funnel; sound is channeled into the ear canal. The eardrum, where the middle ear begins, is at the inside end of the ear canal. (See illustration "The parts of the ear," on pg. 73 of the Teacher's Guide and pg. 36 of the Student Activity Book, in the reading selection in this lesson.)

Sound vibrations cause the eardrum to vibrate, as the students' model eardrums will help them understand. Bones in the middle ear then transfer the vibrations of the eardrum to the fluid-filled inner ear. The movement of the fluid in the inner ear causes hairlike nerve receptors in the inner ear to move. The movement of these receptors causes electrochemical signals to be generated and carried along the auditory nerve to the brain. The brain perceives these signals as sound.

When a sound vibration is produced, sound waves spread out in all directions from the source. Common experience demonstrates that the farther a sound travels from where it originated, the weaker it gets. The closer the eardrum is to the source of a sound, the stronger the vibrations of the eardrum will be. Students can demonstrate this phenomenon by holding a noisemaker near their model eardrum and observing the effect of vibrations caused by the sound.

Many people enjoy loud music and are unaware that it may be harmful to their hearing. The reading selection on "Protecting Our Hearing" and the experience of seeing a vibrating model eardrum can help students take better care of their hearing. You can also refer to the appendix, "Coping with Hearing Impairments," for additional information.

Information on Hearing Health

The following resources provide free information on hearing health:

Information Coordinator, National Institute on Deafness and Other Communication Disorders, National Institutes of Health, Federal Building 31, Room 3c-35, Bethesda, MD 20892. (See the Bibliography in this Teacher's Guide, in the section entitled "Resources for Students," for information on the video *I Love What I Hear.*)

Hearing and Speech Help Line, American Speech-Language-Hearing Association. Call toll-free 1-800-638-8255 between 8:30 a.m. and 4:30 p.m. EST, Monday through Friday.

For a free pamphlet, send a request and self-addressed, stamped envelope to Hearing Protection, American Academy of Otolaryngology, 1 Prince Street, Alexandria, VA 22314.

Materials

For each student
1   science notebook

For every two students
1   plastic tray
1   plastic cup, 284 ml (10 oz)
1   sheet of thin rubber, 15 cm (6 in) square
1   rubber band, No. 64
1   noisemaker
    Pinch of salt or fine sand
1   piece of paper, 10 cm (4 in) square

For the class
- 1 sheet of newsprint
- 1 marker
- 1 pair of scissors

Preparation

1. Decide how you want to dispense the pinch of salt or sand for students to use on their model eardrums. For example, arrange to provide a salt shaker or a small cup of fine sand (or both) for every four students.

2. Cut one small piece of plain paper about 10 cm (4 in) square for each pair of students. During the investigation, they can tear the paper in tiny bits to place on the model eardrum.

Procedure

1. Ask students to think of the work they did in previous lessons and to recall different ways they have observed that vibrations produce sounds. After they have had a few minutes to think, ask them to record their thoughts in their science notebooks.

2. Begin a class list by writing students' ideas on the sheet of newsprint.

3. Let students know that in this activity they will be looking for a way to show that sounds can cause vibrations. They will do this by building a model eardrum and making it vibrate.

4. Distribute a cup, a square sheet of thin rubber, and a rubber band to each pair of students. Ask them to work with their partners to stretch the rubber square tightly over the cup. Suggest that one student hold the cup while the other stretches the rubber square and secures it with a rubber band. (See Figures 8-1(a) and (b).)

Figure 8-1(a)

Making a model eardrum

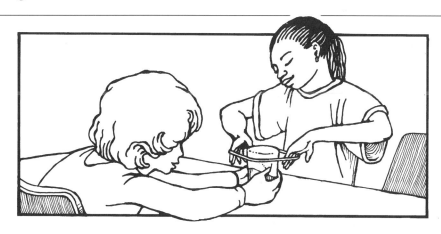

Figure 8-1(b)

The completed model eardrum

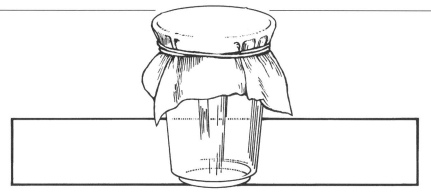

5. After the students have succeeded in attaching the rubber square to the cup with the rubber band, suggest that they pull the edges of the rubber square so that it is stretched as tightly as possible.

6. Then demonstrate how the noisemaker works. (Suggest that students hold it right above the cup and turn the handle rather than twirling it in the air. See Figure 8-2.)

7. Challenge students to use the noisemaker to investigate some ways to show that sounds can cause the model eardrum to vibrate. (For example, salt, fine sand, or small pieces of paper placed on top of the model eardrum will help make the vibrations visible.)

Figure 8-2

Investigating vibrations of the model eardrum

8. Ask students what they think is causing the model eardrum to vibrate. Suggest that they move the noisemaker closer to the model eardrum. What do they observe when the noisemaker and the model eardrum are closer together? What do they observe when the noisemaker is far away from the model eardrum?

9. Ask students to return the materials to the distribution center.

Final Activities

1. Give students an opportunity to share what they have observed with the rest of the class. Encourage them to discuss their ideas about how the eardrum works.

2. Have students read "Protecting Our Hearing," on pgs. 73–74 of the Teacher's Guide and pgs. 36–37 of the Student Activity Book. Ask them to consider the following questions as they read.

   ■ What are some ways to prevent your hearing from being damaged by loud sounds?

   ■ What do you think a hearing aid is used for?

3. Ask students to use words and pictures to describe their ideas about hearing and about the model eardrum in their science notebooks. What are some ways they could tell that the model eardrum was vibrating? What did they observe as the noisemaker got closer to the model eardrum?

Extensions

SCIENCE

1. Most students probably have had their hearing tested at least once. Ask students to discuss what they remember about this experience. Questions such as, "Why do you think you wear headphones when you are having your hearing checked?" or "What do you think the different tones in the test are for?" may help get the discussion started. You may want to explain the process for students who have not been tested or who do not remember. You may even want to ask the school nurse or a hearing specialist to demonstrate the process for the class.

SOCIAL STUDIES

2. Brainstorm with students about what it might be like not to be able to hear. The appendix, "Coping with Hearing Impairments," contains a brief description of the special needs of people who are deaf or who have hearing impairments.

LANGUAGE ARTS   MUSIC

3. Ask students to share their ideas about why the membrane in the ear is called an "eardrum." Suggest that they compare the eardrum with other "drums" they have played or seen someone else play. Students may enjoy constructing their own drums and using them to provide rhythmic accompaniment to stories or to send messages.

SCIENCE

4. Ask students to investigate the kinds of materials that move the most when placed on the model eardrum. (Salt, fine sand, bits of paper, various kinds of breakfast cereal, popcorn, rice, and salt all behave differently.)

SOCIAL STUDIES

5. Challenge students to research how people from different cultures use drums to communicate. Have them share their findings with the class.

SOCIAL STUDIES

6. Invite students to make posters that demonstrate the importance of taking good care of their ears. You may want to share these posters with other classes.

SOCIAL STUDIES

7. Have students research and report on the use of sign language by the deaf or hearing impaired.

Assessment

The **Assessment** section on pgs. 108–9 in Lesson 14 provides strategies for assessing students' understanding of how they hear and how they speak.

Reading Selection

Protecting Our Hearing

Did you know that the thing on the outside of your head that you call your ear is really only part of your ear? The other parts of your ear are inside your head, as the illustration shows. One of these parts is a passageway called the ear canal. At the inside end of the ear canal are the delicate parts of your ear with which you actually hear. Today you made a model of one of these parts—the eardrum.

The eardrum and the other parts of your ear have particular jobs to do, but they all work together. The outer ear, for example, catches sound waves and directs them farther inside your head through the ear canal. The sound waves then hit the eardrum. As you can recall from experimenting with your model, the eardrum vibrates when sound waves hit it. The eardrum needs to vibrate for hearing to take place.

The location of the eardrum inside a person's skull helps protect it from damage. Eardrums are also protected by another safety feature: earwax. This sticky wax collects dust that enters a person's ears. Without earwax, eardrums could become covered with dust; this would interfere with their vibrating when sound hits them.

You may have heard someone say, "Never put anything in your ear that is smaller than your elbow." Of course, you cannot put your elbow in your ear, but it is a good idea not to put any other objects in your ears either. Besides damaging eardrums, objects can get stuck in your ear and interfere with hearing.

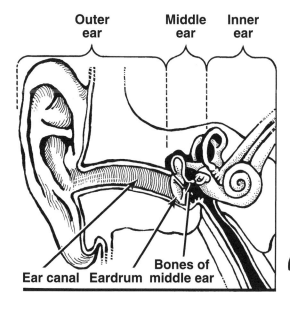

Outer ear   Middle ear   Inner ear

Ear canal   Eardrum   Bones of middle ear

Potentially damaging sound

Another thing that can damage your hearing is loud sounds. Even music that you like to listen to can be harmful if it is too loud. How can you tell if a sound might be loud enough to damage your hearing? If you cannot hear someone talking two feet away from you or if you must raise your voice above the noise around you in order to be heard, it is time to protect your hearing.

One thing you could do to protect your hearing is to move away from the source of the sound. If you can't do that, you can just cover your ears. That is what people do when they work around a lot of noise. Musicians, for example, sometimes wear earplugs to protect their hearing. And at construction sites and airports, you may have seen workers wearing ear protectors that look like headphones.

Even though they may take care of their hearing, people of all ages can have hearing problems. For example, as people age they may lose their ability to hear high-pitched sounds. Both children and adults with hearing problems sometimes use hearing aids. These tiny electronic amplifiers can help make sounds louder, but they cannot always restore normal hearing.

Sometimes we take our hearing for granted. But if we stop for a moment to think of some of the sounds that are important to us—sounds of voices, music, animals, rain, thunder, and many others—we quickly recall how important our hearing is and why we want to take good care of it.

Making Sounds with String

Overview and Objectives

Having used a variety of materials to explore ways to change frequency of vibration and pitch of a sound, students now investigate the sounds produced by a string. Students discover that they can change the pitch of the sounds produced by the string by changing its length. They also find that they can change the pitch by changing the tension, or by using strings of different thicknesses. These discoveries are the basis for the explorations in the next four lessons as students continue to focus on the effects of changing the variables that affect the pitch of the sounds produced by strings.

- Students explore how to produce sounds by causing a string to vibrate.

- Students describe and compare sounds produced by a vibrating string.

- Students investigate different ways that they can change the pitch of the sound produced by the string.

- Students make written records of the results of their investigations.

Background

Strings have been used for thousands of years to produce musical sounds in a wide variety of instruments. Strings have been made from many different materials, including strands of hemp, hair, silk, and the dried intestines of animals (such as sheepgut) woven into strands of great strength.

The strings used for musical instruments must be strong enough to withstand the tension of being strung tightly on the frame of an instrument. The strings also undergo stress when they are played, whether they are plucked, strummed, or bowed. Most instrument strings today are made of either nylon or steel wire—both strong materials. The string used in this lesson is nylon fishing line.

As students will discover in today's lesson, strings by themselves do not make very loud sounds. That is why strings are usually attached to a soundboard, which students will have the opportunity to explore in later lessons. The **soundboard** acts as an amplifier for the sound produced by the vibrations of the strings; it vibrates at the same frequency as the string and makes the sound louder. The tonal quality of a stringed instrument is determined both by the kind of string used and by the shape and construction of the instrument's soundboard.

Because the sounds produced by the vibrating strings in this activity are soft, each student works independently with a piece of string and a string holder. Nevertheless, it is important that students continue to share their observations and ideas with each other.

Figure 9-1

Directions for Preparing String and String Holders

1. Cut one piece of nylon fishing line about 100 cm (39 in) long for each student. Tie a small washer to one end of each piece of string (fishing line).

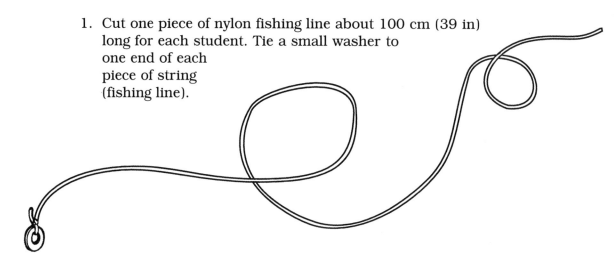

2. To prevent tangling, wrap each string around a piece of cardboard. Make a small slit in the cardboard to help hold the string in place. Begin winding with the washer end in the slit.

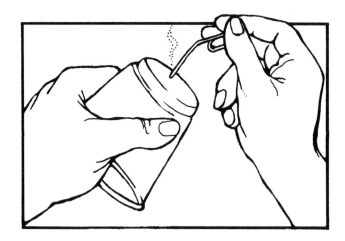

3. Make a tiny hole in the center at the bottom of each plastic cup, using the end of a bent paper clip heated in a candle flame. (Students will thread the string through the hole later in the lesson.)

Materials

For each student

1   science notebook
1   plastic tray
1   piece of string (20-lb nylon fishing line), 100 cm (39 in) long
1   piece of cardboard, 3 × 5 cm (1¼ × 2 in)
1   plastic cup, 261 ml (9 oz), squat
1   small steel washer, No. 10, 12-mm (½-in) diameter
1   unsharpened pencil

For you

1   pair of scissors
1   paper clip
    Candle and matches

Preparation

1. Prepare one piece of string with a holder and cup for each student. Figure 9-1 explains how to do this.

2. Place the materials at the distribution center.

Procedure

1. Ask students to think about a musical instrument that has strings. How would they describe the sound that a string on an instrument makes? What sounds do they think they might make with a string that is not part of an instrument?

2. Let students know that today they will explore sounds made by a single string. Show students the string with the cardboard holder. Then demonstrate the following steps:

    ■ Unwind the string from the piece of cardboard. Take care not to get it tangled.

    ■ Pass the end of the string that does *not* have the washer attached through the hole inside the bottom of the plastic cup.

    ■ Pull the string all the way through the hole in the cup so that the washer is inside the cup.

Figure 9-2

Attaching the string to a plastic cup

3. Challenge students to think of ways they could use this arrangement to make sounds. What could they do with the cup? How could they vibrate the string?

4. Invite students to collect their materials from the distribution center and to find ways to make sounds with the string.

5. After students have tested some of their own ideas, suggest that they try the following:

    ■ Hold the cup against the floor with one foot. Wind the loose end of the string around a pencil and pluck the string with a finger (see Figure 9-3). Change the length of the string by winding more of it around the pencil. What happens to the pitch as the string becomes shorter?

    ■ Have two students work together with one piece of string. Each holds a pencil and winds one end of the string around their pencil. They listen to the changes in pitch as they change the length by winding more around their pencils and plucking the string.

6. Ask students to listen to sounds made by other students. How are the sounds different? How are they the same? Are they using different ways to produce the sounds?

7. Finally, focus students' attention on how the vibrations of the string look. Acknowledge that, while the string's vibrations can be seen, they are not as apparent as the ruler's vibrations were.

8. Ask students to describe their observations. Could they see differences in the string's vibrations when they heard different pitches?

9. Ask students to leave the washer inside the plastic cup, rewind the string around the cardboard, and place it inside the cup before returning these materials to the distribution center.

Figure 9-3

Listening to string sounds

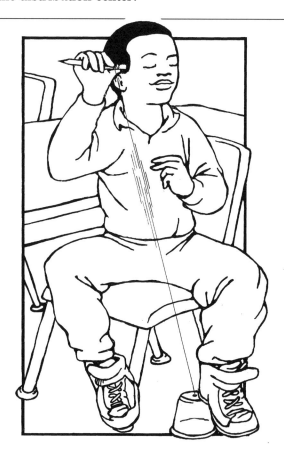

Final Activities

1. To help students reflect on what they discovered, ask them to write in their science notebooks about how strings make sound and to draw pictures to illustrate their discoveries. Allow time for students to share what they found out with the class.

2. Ask students to list in their notebooks any questions they would like to answer about the sounds that strings make.

Extensions

SCIENCE

1. Suggest that students explore making sounds with other types of strings. Some interesting kinds to explore include dental floss, twine, braided fishing line, and sewing thread. What kinds of string seem to work the best?

SCIENCE

2. Bring in some samples of musical instrument strings and place them at a center. Invite students to investigate the sounds each makes.

SCIENCE   LANGUAGE ARTS

3. Have students research how strings for musical instruments are made. See if they can find samples of different kinds of strings.

Assessment

This lesson is the first in a series of four lessons in which students explore how changing the length, tension, and thickness of strings changes the pitch of sounds produced. Although volume is not specifically addressed until Lesson 13, the need to differentiate between pitch and volume is likely to arise in student discussions in all these lessons. Class discussions, notebook entries, record sheets, and work during these lessons can provide information to assess students' understanding of concepts and development of skills.

Concepts

- Sound is produced by vibrating objects.

- Pitch and volume are two characteristics of sound.

- Changing the way an object vibrates can change the pitch and volume of the sound produced.

- Pitch is determined by the frequency of the vibrations; volume is determined by the amplitude of the vibrations.

- Changing the length, tension, or thickness of a string affects the frequency of vibration and, therefore, the pitch of the sound produced.

Skills

- Use of specific examples when comparing and discussing sounds produced.

- Increased detail in notebook entries and on record sheets.

- Continued growth in responsible and safe use of science materials.

- Improvement in organizing and recording results.

- Increased application of previous observations to new experiences.

Changing Pitch by Changing Tension

Overview and Objectives

In Lesson 9, students discovered different ways to produce sound using a piece of string. In this lesson, they focus on the effect of tension on the pitch of the sound produced. Students first explore how to change the tension of the string by building a device that secures the string to a pegboard with an eyebolt. Then they listen to the changes in pitch as the tension changes. These investigations set the stage for students to explore with both length and tension in Lesson 11.

- Students experiment with the production of sound from tightened strings.
- Students compare and discuss their results.
- Students summarize their observations.

Background

The pitch of a sound produced by a string is affected by three variables—the length, tension, and weight or thickness of the string. Although students referred only to the size of the tuning forks and nails when discussing pitch in Lessons 1 and 3, the length and the thickness of those objects also affected the sounds produced. In Lessons 4 through 6, students experimented with sounds made by a vibrating ruler and a slide whistle. They observed that the pitch of the vibrating ruler was dependent upon its length and that the pitch of the slide whistle depended upon the length of the air column.

As students discover in this lesson, greater **tension,** or tightness, in a string of a given length is associated with higher-pitched sounds, and less tension is associated with lower-pitched sounds. However, the pitch of the sound produced by a very loose string may be too low to be audible.

Although the strings used in musical instruments are made of sturdy material, they do stretch over time. This stretching can result in changes in the pitch of the sound produced. Most stringed instruments have tuning pegs, or keys, that allow the tension of each string to be tightened or loosened.

Many students will have heard musicians "tune" their stringed instruments. It is through this tuning process—tightening or loosening of strings—that musicians are able to create the pitch desired for each string on their instrument.

Materials

For each student

1   science notebook

For every two students

1   plastic tray

1   pegboard, 15 × 45 × 0.6 cm (6 × 18 × ¼ in), with holes slightly larger than 4-mm (³⁄₁₆-in) diameter, to fit eyebolts

1   piece of 20-lb nylon fishing line, 60 cm (24 in) long

1   eyebolt, 3.75 cm (1½ in) long, with 4-mm (³⁄₁₆-in) diameter

2   small steel washers, No. 10, 12-mm (½-in) diameter

1   wing nut to fit eyebolt

Preparation

1.   Practice assembling the pegboard harp as shown in the **Student Instructions for Assembling a One-Stringed Pegboard Harp,** on pg. 86 in the Teacher's Guide and pg. 45 in the Student Activity Book.

2.   Arrange materials for easy collection at the distribution center.

Figure 10-1

Materials

Procedure

1.   Ask students to think of ways, in addition to those they explored in earlier lessons, to make a sound have a higher or lower pitch. Have them record their ideas in their science notebooks.

2.   After students have exchanged ideas in small groups, bring the whole class together to share ideas.

3.   Now invite students to think about their experience producing sounds with string in Lesson 9. Were they able to make high-pitched sounds? Low-pitched sounds? How did they change the string to make different sounds?

4. To introduce the focus of this lesson, ask students how they think the sound will change if they stretch a string tight. Then show them the pegboard harp that you made and let them see how the eyebolt changes the tension.

5. Have students collect their materials and assemble the pegboard harp according to the **Student Instructions** on pg. 45 of their Student Activity Books.

6. Challenge students, working in pairs, to listen while their partner tightens the eyebolt and plucks the string. Then have the partners change roles and repeat the activity so that each student has the chance to listen to the full range of pitch that the string can produce.

7. Ask students to leave the string attached to the pegboard harp and to return all materials to the distribution center.

Final Activities

1. Allow students time to record their observations and ideas in their science notebooks. Remind them that they can also use drawings.

    They can begin by focusing on the following questions:

    ■   When you turned the eyebolt, what happened to the string?

    ■   What happened to the pitch when you tightened the string?

2. Ask students to share their ideas about the tightness, or tension, of the string and about pitch.

Extensions

1. Invite someone who is taking lessons on a stringed instrument to demonstrate how the strings on the instrument are tuned.

2. Invite a piano tuner to visit the classroom and explain his or her work to the class.

Student Instructions for Assembling a One-Stringed Pegboard Harp

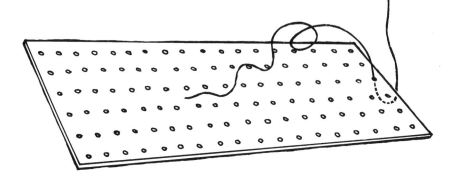

1. Tie one end of the string to a hole at one end of the pegboard.

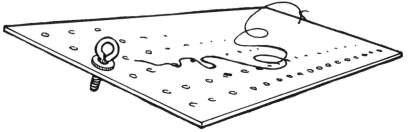

2. Place one washer on the eyebolt and run the eyebolt through a hole at the other end of the pegboard. (The washer will be on the top surface of the pegboard.)

3. Secure the end of the eyebolt on the underside of the pegboard with another washer and a wing nut.

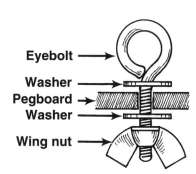

Eyebolt
Washer
Pegboard
Washer
Wing nut

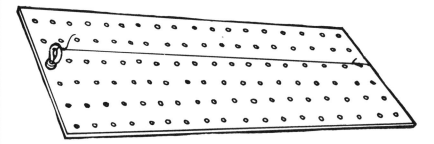

4. Tie the loose end of the string to the eyebolt. Turn the eyebolt to tighten or loosen the string.

Tuning a Stringed Instrument

Overview and Objectives

Students now build on their earlier experiences with pitch by varying both length and tension to produce sounds with a range of different pitches on the pegboard harp. After adding more strings to the harp they made in Lesson 10, they explore ways to change the pitch of the sounds produced by changing the length and the tension of the strings.

- Students build a pegboard harp with several strings.

- Students experiment with ways to change the pitch of the sounds produced.

- Students compare and discuss their results.

- Students summarize their observations in writing and with drawings.

Background

The harp is one of the world's oldest stringed instruments. Remains of harps have been found in Egyptian tombs that are 6,000 years old. Harps come in different sizes, they are made of various materials, and the number of strings they have varies, but they have a common shape. Moreover, all are played by plucking the strings. The length of the strings can vary from about 7 or 8 cm (about 3 in) to more than 150 cm (60 in).

The pitch of the sound produced by each harp string is determined by both the length of the string and its tension. As students learned in earlier lessons, the longer a string is, the lower the basic pitch of the sound produced. However, when that same string is looser, the pitch of its sound is even lower. The harp player can adjust the pitch of each string by turning its tuning peg to tighten or loosen it.

Although students will not investigate the effect of the weight or thickness of the string on pitch in this lesson, some of the strings on a real harp do have different thicknesses. The longest strings are thicker and heavier than the other strings, which makes the longer strings even lower in pitch. Students have an opportunity to investigate this last variable in Lessons 12 and 13.

Materials

For each student
   1   science notebook

For every two students
   1   pegboard harp (from Lesson 10)
   1   plastic tray

3   eyebolts, 3.75 cm (1½ in) long, with 4-mm (³⁄₁₆-in) diameter
6   small steel washers, No. 10, 12-mm (½-in) diameter
3   wing nuts to fit eyebolts
3   pieces of string (20-lb nylon fishing line), 60 cm (24 in) long

Preparation   Arrange materials at the distribution center.

Procedure

1. Invite students to think about their experience producing sounds with string in Lesson 10. How were they able to make high-pitched sounds? Low-pitched sounds?

2. Ask if any students have heard or seen a harp being played. If so, invite them to describe the harp. If not, direct them to the picture of the harp in Figure 11-1, below, and on pg. 48 of the Student Activity Book. Then let them know that today they will add more strings to their own harps.

3. Have students collect their materials and add strings to their harps, according to the **Student Instructions for Assembling a Four-Stringed Pegboard Harp,** on pg. 92 of the Teacher's Guide and pg. 50 of the Student Activity Book.

Figure 11-1

A harp

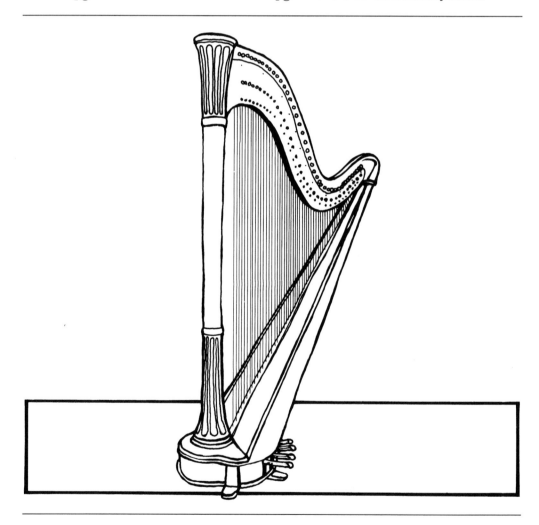

Figure 11-2

*Investigating
string tension
and pitch*

4. Suggest that one student listen while his or her partner plucks the strings. (See Figure 11-2.) Then the partners should switch roles and repeat the activity so that each student has the opportunity to listen to the full range of pitches the stringed instrument can produce.

5. Challenge students to change the pitch of the sounds produced by adjusting the tension of each string.

Management Tip: Remind the class to stay very quiet while working on this activity. If students still have difficulty hearing different pitches, arrange for some to work in the hall.

6. Ask students to untie the strings from the pegboard harps, but to leave the eyebolts attached and to return the materials to the distribution center.

Final Activities

1. Allow students time to record their observations and ideas in their science notebooks. Remind them that they can also use drawings.

2. Ask students to share their ideas about how both the length and the tightness of the strings affected the pitch. They can consider the following questions:

   ■ Which strings produced sounds with the highest pitches? The lowest pitches?

   ■ What happens to the pitch when you tighten the string? When you loosen it?

   ■ What might you do to produce a high pitch from a long string?

Extensions

MUSIC

1. Encourage students to research how strings for musical instruments are made.

MUSIC

2. Invite a harp player to visit class and demonstrate the range of pitches the instrument can produce.

Student Instructions for Assembling a Four-Stringed Pegboard Harp

1. Using the harp with one string from Lesson 10, place three additional eyebolts with washers and wing nuts at the end of the pegboard where the first eyebolt is attached.

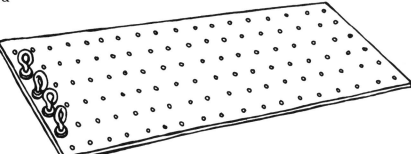

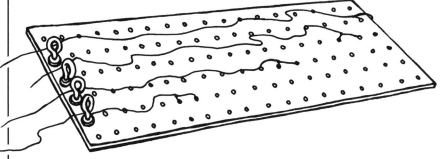

2. Tie pieces of string in holes at the end of the pegboard opposite the eyebolts. Choose holes that will allow the strings to be of four different lengths.

3. Tie the loose end of the strings in the eyebolts.

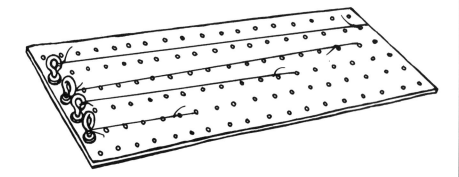

How Do Different Strings Sound?

Overview and Objectives

Having explored the connection between tension and pitch, students now extend their investigations to explore the effect of changing the thickness of the string. They discover that strings of the same length but different thicknesses can produce sounds with different pitches. Investigating the effects of changing the tension of these strings reinforces students' previous discoveries.

- Students explore and describe the sounds produced by vibrating strings with different thicknesses.

- Students compare and discuss ways to change pitch.

- Students make written records of their investigations.

Background

The violin family of stringed instruments includes the violin, viola, cello, and bass. Each has four strings stretched across a bridge to transmit the sound to the resonating box. The shape of these instruments is very much alike, but their size varies considerably. When listening to the four instruments together, one quickly hears that the very long strings of the bass produce much deeper sounds than those from the shorter strings of the violin. Previous lessons have focused on this relationship of length and pitch.

However, listening to just one of these instruments at a time, one notices the wide range of pitch produced by four strings that are all the *same* length. This range of pitch is possible because the strings are of different weights and thicknesses. The heavier and thicker the string, the lower the sound it can produce. Therefore, even though the vibrating length of the four strings is the same when they are open (not pressed down with a finger), the string that is the heaviest and thickest will produce the sound with the lowest pitch.

There is a visible difference in the thickness of the four pieces of fishing line used in today's lesson, and they will produce four distinctly different pitches when they are attached to the pegboard harp and tightened so that they have about the same tension. This makes it easy for students to discover the connection between thickness and pitch. They will see that the thinnest piece of fishing line produces the sound with the highest pitch.

To perform a "fair test," students need to make the tension of all four pieces of fishing line about the same. To do this, they tighten one string until it is taut; then, feeling how taut that string is, they adjust the tightness of the other three to match. Holding the tension constant is difficult with the pegboard arrangement, so it is important to discuss this idea of a fair test and to encourage students to attempt to adjust all strings to about the same tightness. One technique that can be used is to tighten each string just until there is no slack; then turn each eyebolt the same number of half turns to increase the tension equally.

Materials

For every two students

1   pegboard harp (from Lesson 11)
1   60-cm (24-in) piece of 8-lb nylon fishing line
1   60-cm (24-in) piece of 30-lb nylon fishing line
1   60-cm (24-in) piece of 50-lb nylon fishing line
1   60-cm (24-in) piece of 60-lb nylon fishing line

Preparation

Place materials at the distribution center for easy collection by the students. Figure 12-1 suggests one possible arrangement.

Figure 12-1

Arrangement for distributing materials

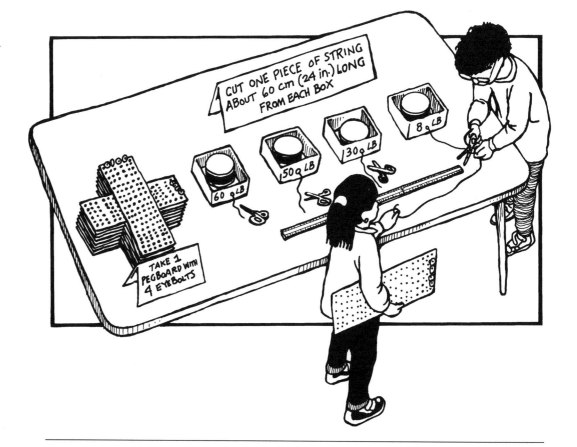

Procedure

1.   Ask students to describe sounds they produced with the strings in the three previous lessons. Invite them to share their ideas about the differences in pitch that were produced when they plucked the long and short strings.

2.   Now ask students to think about the string they have been using. How do they think a thicker string would sound? A thinner string?

3.   Challenge students to think about how they might make sounds with just a string.

4. Let students know that they will investigate answers to all these questions today using strings that have different thicknesses. Have pairs of students collect their materials from the distribution center.

5. Invite students to find ways to make sounds with just the string. After they have experimented for a few minutes, suggest, if necessary, that they stretch a string close to a partner's ear and snap it quickly, as shown in Figure 12-2.

Figure 12-2

Snapping the string and listening to pitch

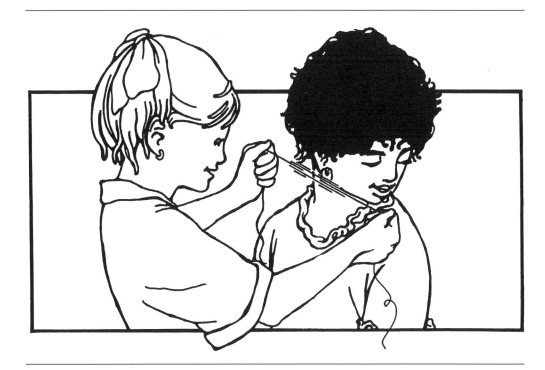

6. Next, focus students' attention on how the strings look. Can they see differences in their thickness? Which string produced the sound with the highest pitch? Which string produced the sound with the lowest pitch?

7. Then have each pair of students attach the four strings to their pegboard harp. Suggest that they attach the strings in sequence from thickest to thinnest.

8. Challenge students to investigate how strings of different thicknesses can produce different pitches. Before they begin, discuss with them the importance of having about the same tension in all four strings. Ask for their ideas on how they can make the tension about the same.

9. Ask students to return their materials to the distribution center.

Final Activities

1. To help students reflect on what they discovered, ask them first to write in their science notebooks about how strings make sounds and then ask them to draw pictures to illustrate their discoveries. Allow time for them to share what they found out with the class.

2. Ask students to list in their notebooks any questions they would like to answer about the sounds that strings make.

Extensions

| MUSIC |

1. Suggest that students read about the history of stringed instruments in a book such as *Music,* by Neil Ardley. Suggest that they make a poster or time line to illustrate and share what they learn.

| SCIENCE |

2. Invite students to create an experiment to test the breaking point of the fishing line used in this lesson. Help them acquire the materials they need to conduct their experiments.

| MUSIC |

3. Play a tape of a piece of music performed by a string ensemble and invite students to describe their impressions of the music.

| MUSIC | | MATHEMATICS |

4. Have students research the variety of stringed instruments to determine the number of strings most commonly used. The class can organize the information into a graph.

Making Louder Sounds from Strings

Overview and Objectives

Having explored the effect of the length, tension, and thickness of strings on pitch, students are ready to apply what they know about all three variables as they further investigate how they can change the pitch of sounds. This lesson introduces them to the use of a bridge and soundboard to increase the volume of the sound produced. At the end of the lesson, brainstorming on other ways to increase the volume of the sound produced sets the stage for the unit's culminating activity, in which students are challenged to design their own device to demonstrate what they have learned.

- Students discuss how they have changed the pitch of the sounds produced by strings.

- Students explore the effect of adding a bridge to their stringed instrument.

- Students compare and discuss ways to change pitch.

- Students make written records of their investigations.

Background

Students have investigated the sounds produced by different lengths, tensions, and thicknesses of strings. However, the sounds that have been produced so far have not been very loud.

Actual stringed instruments can produce louder sounds because the strings rest on a **bridge,** an upright piece of wood, which is connected to a thin soundboard. The vibrations of the string cause the bridge to vibrate, which in turn vibrates the soundboard. The soundboard is actually the wooden body of the instrument. Since the soundboard has a far larger surface than that of the strings, it is much more effective in producing sound waves. The cavity of the instrument's body also reflects the sound waves back and forth within it, making them louder.

The pegboard harp that students have used has allowed them to change the pitch but not to increase the volume of the sounds produced. The wooden bridge introduced in this lesson will allow the pegboard to act as a soundboard, vibrating to produce louder sounds. However, the first observation students will probably make after adding the bridge is that the tension of the strings increases.

Adding a wooden box, or body, to their pegboard harp would increase loudness even more. In Lesson 15, students will be encouraged to bring in a variety of boxes. These and other containers that they may suggest can be used as the "bodies" of the stringed instruments they may wish to construct in Lessons 15 and 16.

Materials

For each student
1 science notebook

For every two students
1 pegboard harp (from Lesson 12)
1 wooden bridge, 2.5 × 15 × 0.65 cm (1 × 6 × ⁵⁄₁₆ in)

For the class
2 sheets of newsprint
Markers

Preparation

1. Place materials at the distribution center.

2. On one sheet of newsprint, write "Ways We Produced Sounds with Different Pitches." Post this chart for use during the class brainstorming session. On the second sheet, write "Materials We Could Use to Make Instruments."

Procedure

1. Ask students to think about changes they made in the strings that resulted in sounds with different pitches. Then record their ideas on the class brainstorming chart, "Ways We Produced Sounds with Different Pitches."

2. Let students know that today they will investigate ways to increase the volume of the sound produced by their stringed instruments. Show them the piece of wood; refer to it as being like the bridge on a violin. (Refer students to Figure 13-1 in their Student Activity Books for an illustration of a violin.)

3. Have students collect their materials from the distribution center. Challenge them to experiment with the position of the bridge as well as with adjusting the tension and length of the strings.

4. Focus students' attention on how the vibrations of each string look when they pluck it. Can they see differences in the vibrations after adding the bridge? Suggest that they also try pulling back farther on each string. Does this change the way the string vibrates? Does it increase the volume?

5. After students have discussed their ideas with others, allow time for them to test ideas suggested by other students.

6. Ask students to return their materials to the distribution center.

Figure 13-1

Pegboard
harp with
a bridge

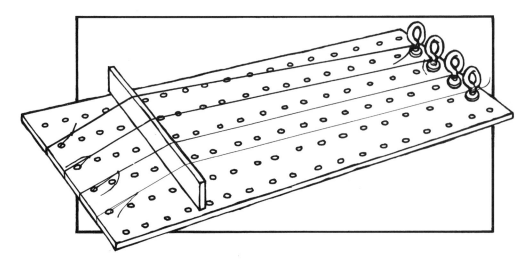

Final Activities

1. To help students reflect on what they have discovered, ask them to write in their science notebooks about how the bridge affects the sounds produced and then to draw pictures to illustrate their discoveries.

2. Ask students to think of materials they could use as the body of a stringed instrument. Record their ideas on the chart labeled, "Materials We Could Use to Make Instruments." Then encourage them to think of other instruments they could make to demonstrate what they now know about how sounds are produced.

Extensions

MUSIC

1. Suggest that students read books, such as *What Instrument Is This?*, by Rosmarie Hausherr, about instruments in the stringed instrument group.

MUSIC

2. Invite a string player to visit the class. Encourage him or her to allow students to explore similarities and differences between two stringed instruments of different sizes that are played with a bow—for example, a violin and a cello.

MUSIC   SOCIAL STUDIES

3. Invite members of a bluegrass band to play their instruments—for example, a fiddle, banjo, guitar, mandolin, or washtub bass—for the class. Ask the musicians to tell students about the origins of bluegrass music in the United States.

Making Sounds with Air and Strings: The Human Vocal Cords

Overview and Objectives

In Lesson 8, students used a model eardrum to investigate hearing. This lesson again focuses students' attention on themselves as they investigate how vocal cords produce sounds. After constructing a rubber band model of the vocal cords, students apply what they now know about producing sound and about ways to change pitch as they experiment with the model. Through discussion of the reading selection, they learn more about the role of the human vocal cords in the production of speech.

- Students investigate sounds produced with rubber bands.

- Students use rubber bands to make a model of human vocal cords.

- Students record and discuss observations and questions about sounds produced with the model vocal cords.

- Students read to learn more about how people produce sounds with their vocal cords.

- Students compare vibrations of their own vocal cords with those of their models.

Background

In this lesson, students construct a model of human vocal cords from rubber bands and a plastic cup. (See Figure 14-1.) Blowing on the stretched rubber bands in the model vocal cords provides a rough approximation of the way human vocal cords produce sound.

Figure 14-1

Model vocal cords

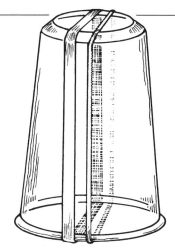

Sound is produced by the human voice as air moves through the tightened **vocal cords.** These cords are folds of muscle that can completely close the opening between the lungs and the throat. For normal breathing, the folds relax and the opening permits air to move freely. For speech, muscles in the throat tighten the cords and partially close the opening. Muscles in the chest and abdomen then create enough air pressure in the lungs to force air through the folds. Just as the neck of a balloon can vibrate and produce sound as air rushes out, the vocal cords vibrate as the air is forced through them. This vibration produces a sound. To refine this sound into speech, the throat and tongue alter the shape of the mouth cavity and control the way the air flows and vibrates.

The reading selection "Making Sounds with Our Vocal Cords," on pgs. 110–11 in the Teacher's Guide and pgs. 60–61 in the Student Activity Book, contains additional information on this topic. A diagram in the reading selection illustrates the human vocal cords.

In the model that the students make, the rubber bands can be made to vibrate, one at a time, by blowing across them. Students will discover that blowing on the longer segment of a rubber band will produce a sound with a lower pitch than that produced by a shorter segment. They also discover that a higher-pitched sound can be produced by increasing the tension in the rubber band. When discussing the reading selection, students can see the relationship of the length— that is, the longer segment of the rubber bands on their model—to growth and age. They also can see the relationship between the tension of the rubber band and the tightening of muscles in speaking.

Materials

For each student

- 1 science notebook
- 1 plastic tray
- 1 plastic "Jumbo" drinking straw
- 1 rubber band, No. 33
- 1 rubber band, No. 64
- 1 plastic cup, 284 ml (10 oz)

Preparation

1. Arrange the materials for collection at the distribution center.

2. Before beginning this lesson, investigate the model vocal cords yourself. Try out the following hints, which may be useful for students who have difficulty getting the rubber bands to vibrate when they blow on them:

   - Adjust the rubber bands by moving them slightly off center.

   - Place the cup on its side and blow on the rubber bands along the side of the cup.

   - Take rests between breaths and blow gently to avoid becoming light-headed.

Procedure

1. Ask students to think about the following questions:

   - How are rubber bands like strings?

   - How are they different?

   - How could sounds be produced with rubber bands?

2. Have students record their ideas in their notebooks and then discuss the questions in small groups.

3. Have each student collect a cup and the two different rubber bands. Encourage them to test their ideas and make sounds with the rubber bands.

4. Distribute the straws to students. Challenge them to try to produce a sound by blowing gently through the straw onto the rubber bands, as shown in Figure 14-2. Allow time for students to experiment with ways to produce different sounds.

Figure 14-2

Blowing on a rubber band to produce sound

 Management Tip: Have a box of tissues handy when students experiment with blowing through the straws, since saliva often gets blown through the straws together with air. This happens less if students blow gently, which they should do to avoid becoming light-headed. In addition, blowing gently may produce stronger vibrations than blowing harder.

5. Ask students to discard the straws and return the other materials to their storage area.

6. Have students record their findings in their notebooks by writing or drawing about them, or both. To focus their thoughts, use questions such as these:

■ How do you think the sound was produced?

■ What are some ways that you were able to change the pitch of the sound?

Final Activities

1. Explain to students that inside the throat are vocal cords that are similar to the stretched rubber bands they have been working with. Tell them that muscles in the throat pull the vocal cords tight to make higher sounds and relax them to make lower sounds.

Figure 14-3

Finding out how vibrating vocal cords feel

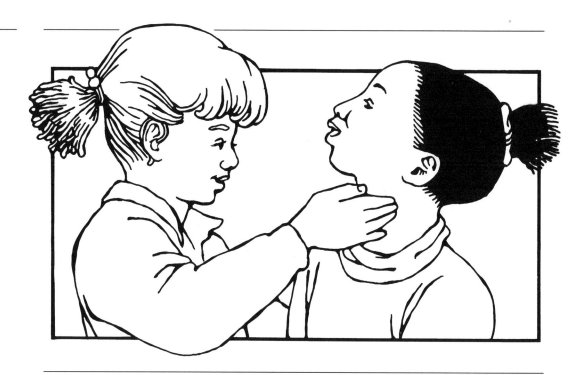

2. Ask each student to place one hand gently against another student's throat. Have the second student say "Hello" first in a low voice and then in a high voice. (See Figure 14-3.)

3. Have students repeat Step 2, this time asking them to feel their own throats.

4. Ask students to read "Making Sounds with Our Vocal Cords," on pgs. 110–11 of the Teacher's Guide and pgs. 60–61 of the Student Activity Book, to learn more about how people produce sounds.

5. After the class has finished reading, discuss the following questions:

   ■ How are human vocal cords similar to your rubber band model?

   ■ How are they different?

Extensions

$\boxed{\textbf{SCIENCE}}$

1. Challenge students to conduct experiments using rubber bands of different sizes or cups of different sizes.

$\boxed{\textbf{SCIENCE}}$

2. Invite students to research how some animals without vocal cords communicate with sounds.

Assessment

To assess students' understanding of how they hear and speak, review their notebook entries from this lesson and Lesson 8, "Making a Model Eardrum." Before students begin their discussion, refer to the experiments of these two lessons. Allow time for students to relate the experiences from this lesson to those in Lesson 8. During the discussion, listen for understanding of the following.

- The models are similar to, yet different from, the real ear and vocal cords.

- The human ear has a membrane that vibrates when sound reaches it.

- Ears can be damaged by very loud sounds.

- Sound is produced by the human vocal cords when air moves through the tightened cords.

Students' growth in the following skills should also be assessed at this point.

Performing Experiments

- How do students work together in pairs and in groups?

- Do students take responsibility for collecting and returning their materials to the distribution center?

- How well do students follow directions for safe use of materials?

- How do students exchange information and ideas?

Recordkeeping

- Is every entry dated?

- How complete are recorded entries?

- Are sketches included as part of the record of an experiment?

- Do summaries recorded reflect actual results?

Discussions

- Are students able to communicate their findings?

- Do students compare and question results of the ideas of others?

- Do students refer to their records of experiments and readings in discussions?

Reading Selection

Making Sounds with Our Vocal Cords

Crickets chirp, rabbits thump, and birds sing. Animals make sounds to tell each other things. Some animals, like dogs, make sounds in their throats the way people do, although they cannot speak words or make as many different sounds as people can.

"But how *do* people make sounds?" you may wonder. "How do I make the sounds that I hear when I talk or sing?"

To make these sounds—to speak, sing, laugh, or shout—you use your vocal cords. They are in a place in your throat called your voice box, as the drawing shows.

You can find your voice box by locating your Adam's apple. Your Adam's apple is a piece of tissue (cartilage) inside your throat at the front of your voice box. To find your Adam's apple, gently touch the front of your neck at about the middle of your throat. Your Adam's apple will feel like a bump. Do not worry if you cannot find it. If you can speak, you definitely have a voice box.

Now look at the drawing again. You will see that your voice box is at the top of the tube called the windpipe (trachea). Your windpipe goes down to your lungs. When you are ready to speak or sing, you send air from your lungs up your windpipe. This happens so fast you usually don't even know you are doing it. The air moves up your windpipe, through your voice box, and out of your mouth. When the air passes between the vocal cords in your voice box, it makes them vibrate, and you hear the sound of your voice.

Location of the vocal cords

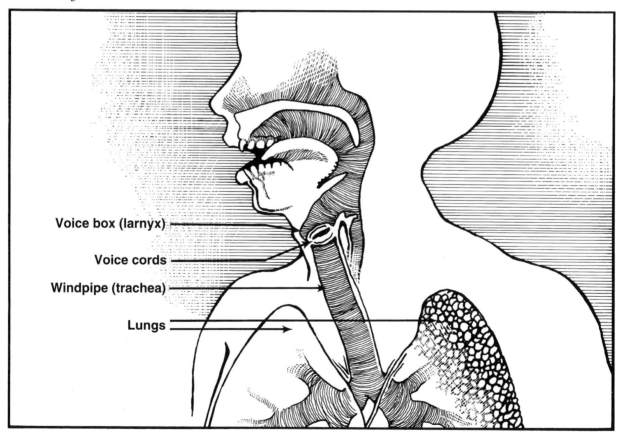

Voice box (larnyx)

Voice cords

Windpipe (trachea)

Lungs

Air also passes between your vocal cords each time you breathe in or out. But the vocal cords are open so that they do not vibrate when you are just breathing. When you want to speak or sing, your vocal cords tighten up and move closer together. These two pictures show the difference.

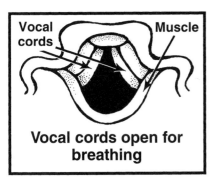

Vocal cords open for breathing

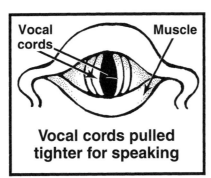

Vocal cords pulled tighter for speaking

You made a model of your vocal cords today. The rubber bands in your model stretch like the vocal cords in your voice box. The rubber bands make higher sounds when they are stretched tighter, and your vocal cords make higher sounds when they are stretched tighter.

Adult women's vocal cords are about 11 millimeters (about one-half inch) long. Adult men's vocal cords are typically longer. They are about 15 millimeters (about two-thirds of an inch) long. Adult men usually have deeper voices than women do. When a boy is about 12 years old and his voice begins to change, his vocal cords grow longer and become thicker. That is what makes his voice sound deeper.

You may have noticed that sometimes your voice sounds "froggy" or "hoarse." This happens when your voice box becomes inflamed or swollen because you have used your voice a lot or you were sick. This condition is called **laryngitis** (lair-in-jite-us). The name comes from the word **larynx** (lair-inks). Larynx is the scientific name for voice box. People who have laryngitis usually are able to speak only in a soft voice. This gives their larynx a chance to recover.

You may have wondered why your voice sounds different from your friends' voices. It has its own special sound because of the length and thickness of your vocal cords and the size and shape of your chest, throat, nose, mouth, and the bones in your head. No one else's head and chest are exactly the same size and shape as yours, so no one else's voice sounds just like yours.

What Have We Learned about Sound?

Overview and Objectives

This lesson is the first of a two-part application assessment. Students are presented with the challenge of designing a musical instrument or creating a device to show what they have learned about how sound is produced and changed, how it travels, and how it is received by the human ear. The planning process requires students to reflect on and apply previous learning to design their instruments or devices. As students test their inventions, they will be applying the process skill of modifying and improving their designs, which will expand their understanding of the process of design. Students complete the assessment by constructing, testing, and presenting their projects in Lesson 16.

- Students review and reflect on what they have learned about sound.

- Students brainstorm ways they could demonstrate what they have learned.

- Students plan their presentations.

- Students design and begin building instruments or devices that apply what they know about sound.

Background

Throughout the unit, students have engaged in a variety of experiences and activities that focused their ears, eyes, and minds on the phenomenon of sound in their lives. They have experimented with various physical aspects of sound and have read about and discussed the importance and meaning of different types of sound. Students are now invited to draw on what they have learned to plan and make a presentation on some aspect of sound.

The lesson is designed to encourage students to be creative both in interpreting the challenge and in designing their inventions and presentations. Students' ways of addressing the challenge, as well as their plans, will provide information for assessing their conceptual understanding and their understanding of the process of design. Students work together in small groups to plan and carry out a final project. However, each individual student completes his or her own record sheets pertaining to the group project.

Many groups will probably choose to design and build a musical instrument. As students plan and refine their inventions, they engage in a process referred to as **technological design.** This means that as they create their plans, they will evaluate the results and improve the plans.

You will want to encourage students to analyze their plans to find ways to make them better. While they are constructing their instruments or devices, you can use questioning strategies to stimulate their ideas about such issues as how to stabilize tension in strings, how to increase the variety of sounds produced, or how to improve the appearance of their inventions.

Ideas for several types of projects are listed in **Procedure,** Step 7. The intent of the lesson is not to produce research papers but to allow a creative means for you and your students to demonstrate and evaluate their growth in understanding sound.

Materials

For each student

1   copy of **Record Sheet 15-A: Design Sheet**
1   copy of **Record Sheet 15-B: Presentation Planning Sheet**
1   science notebook

For each group of two or three students

1   copy of three blackline masters, **Ideas for Stringed Instruments, Ideas for Wind Instruments,** and **Ideas for Chimes**

For the class

Materials from the kit
Assorted books on sound and on musical instruments
Cardboard tubes and boxes (such as tissue boxes, shoe boxes, candy boxes)
String, rubber bands, paper clips
Straws
Tape and glue
1   sheet of newsprint
Markers

Preparation

1. Duplicate one copy of **Record Sheet 15-A: Design Sheet** and **Record Sheet 15-B: Presentation Planning Sheet** for each student.

2. For each group of two or three students, make one copy of the three blackline masters, **Ideas for Stringed Instruments, Ideas for Wind Instruments,** and **Ideas for Chimes,** on pgs. 119–21 of the Teacher's Guide.

3. Collect several books on sound, musical instruments, hearing, and related topics for students to use. (The Bibliography lists suggested readings.)

4. Collect a variety of materials that students might use for their projects. These should include boxes of assorted sizes and shapes, cardboard tubes from paper towel and toilet tissue rolls, strings, small pieces of wood, and rubber bands.

5. Arrange the materials at the distribution center.

Procedure

1. Organize the class in working groups of two or three students each.

2. Ask students what they now know about sound. Use the following specific questions to focus their thoughts as they review their science notebooks.

    ■ How is sound produced?

    ■ What materials does sound travel through?

    ■ How does the ear work?

    ■ How do human vocal cords produce sound?

- What are some ways we can change the pitch of sounds?

- What are some ways we can change the volume of sounds?

3. Encourage students to share some of their ideas with their group.

4. Remind students of the instruments they made in earlier lessons. What were they able to demonstrate with those instruments? Now challenge the class to think of ways they could demonstrate some of the other things they have learned about sound.

5. Invite students to share their ideas as you record them on a class brainstorming chart.

6. Distribute the blackline masters to each group of students. Explain that these are drawings of some instruments that students have made. Let the groups know that these drawings, together with the exploration questions on the blackline masters, may help them generate their own ideas and plan their own projects.

7. Provide time for each group to decide on a project and begin its plans. Here are some ideas in case students are having trouble getting started with a plan:

- Make an oral presentation with a poster to show which parts of different musical instruments vibrate to make sounds.

- Design a musical instrument and demonstrate how to tune it.

- Design a way other than those used in Lesson 2 to show how sound travels. Make a paper cup telephone, for example, and explain why a person can hear better through the telephone than through air.

- Demonstrate the sound-insulating properties of various materials. For example, wrap an alarm clock in different materials. How loud does the tick or alarm sound with each one?

8. Point out the collection of materials you have assembled at the distribution center. Invite students to explore with the materials as they are planning. Remind them that they can bring in additional materials from home.

Final Activities

1. Distribute one copy of **Record Sheet 15-A: Design Sheet** and **Record Sheet 15-B: Presentation Planning Sheet** to each student. Review these sheets and how to use them.

Figure 15-1

Planning an instrument or device

2. Let students know that in the next lesson they will be able to complete their devices and demonstrate them for the rest of the class. Discuss the procedure you will use for these demonstrations (see **Preparation,** Step 2, in Lesson 16). Remind students that they must also complete the Presentation Planning Sheet (Record Sheet 15-B) and be ready to answer questions about their projects.

Note: You may need to allow several class periods for students to complete their projects and presentations. You may choose to integrate this activity with language arts instruction.

Record Sheet 15–A

Name: _____

Date: _____

Design Sheet

1. Write the name of the instrument or device you are planning to construct.

   _____

2. What does this invention do?

   _____

   _____

   _____

3. What materials will you need to make this instrument or device?

   _____

   _____

   _____

4. How does this instrument or device demonstrate what you have learned about sound?

   _____

   _____

   _____

5. Draw and label a sketch of your invention.

Record Sheet 15–B

Name: _____

Date: _____

Presentation Planning Sheet

1. Write down the ideas you want to present.

    _____

    _____

    _____

    _____

    _____

    _____

    _____

    _____

2. Outline how you will present these ideas.

    _____

    _____

    _____

    _____

    _____

    _____

    _____

    _____

Ideas for Stringed Instruments

African Gourd Harp

Plastic container

Bow and Violin/Banjo

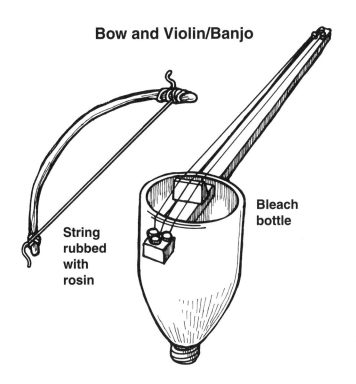

String rubbed with rosin

Bleach bottle

String Bass

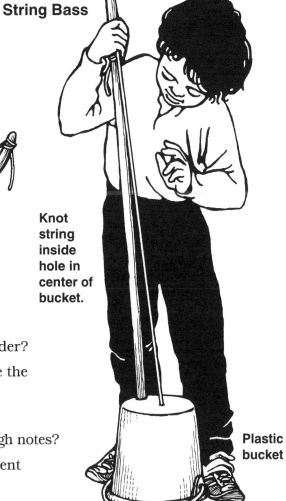

Knot string inside hole in center of bucket.

Plastic bucket

African Gourd-Bow Instrument

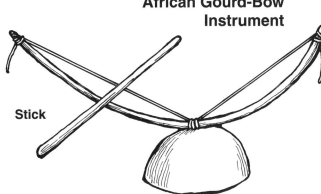

Stick

Ideas to Explore

- How can you make a stringed instrument sound louder?

- How do different materials for the sound box change the instrument's sound?

- What materials produce the most pleasing sound?

- What kinds of strings work best for low notes? For high notes?

- How do bridges made of different materials or different shapes affect the sound?

Ideas for Wind Instruments

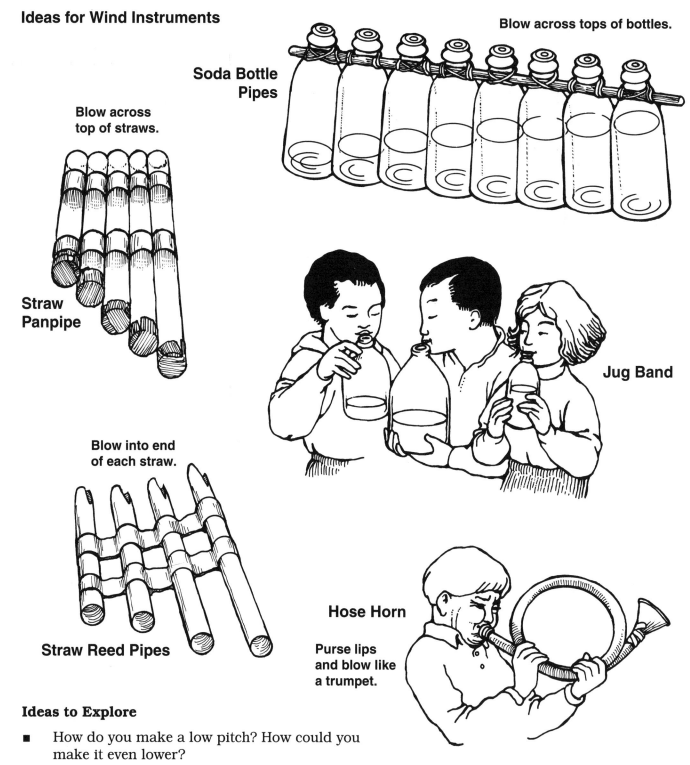

Blow across tops of bottles.

Soda Bottle Pipes

Blow across top of straws.

Straw Panpipe

Jug Band

Blow into end of each straw.

Straw Reed Pipes

Hose Horn

Purse lips and blow like a trumpet.

Ideas to Explore

- How do you make a low pitch? How could you make it even lower?

- What happens to the pitch of a horn if you change the position of your lips?

- How can you make the instrument sound louder?

- How can you show what part of the instrument is vibrating to produce sounds?

- How many different materials could you use to make your instrument? How do you think the different materials would affect its sound?

Ideas for Chimes

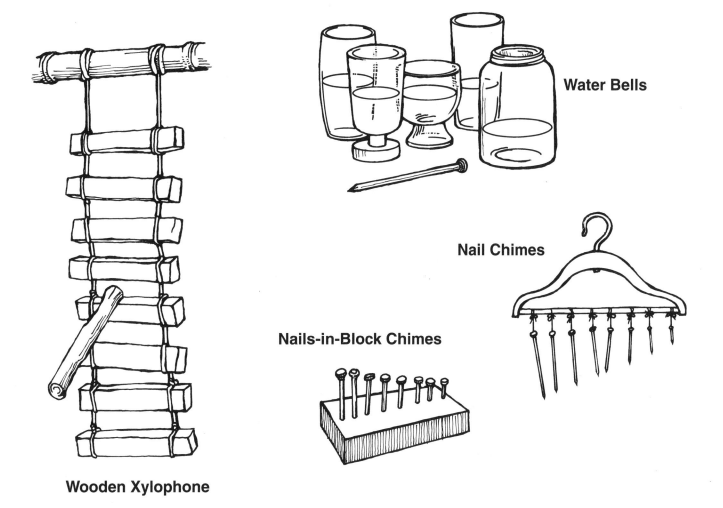

Water Bells

Nail Chimes

Nails-in-Block Chimes

Wooden Xylophone

Flowerpot Bells

Ideas to Explore

■ Which of the chimes or bells in the set produces the highest pitch and why?

■ What would you change to make the pitch even higher?

■ Which material makes the most pleasing sound?

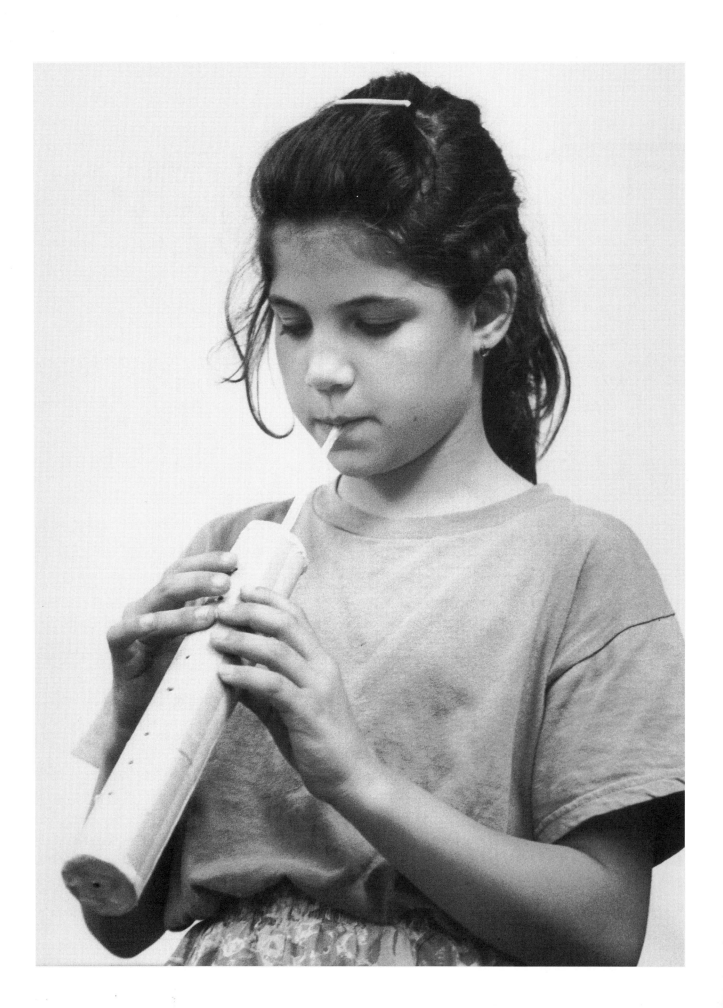

Sharing What We Have Learned

Overview and Objectives

In this final lesson, students construct and test the instruments or devices they designed in Lesson 15. When they share these with the class, their descriptions and discussions will provide you with information for assessing what they have learned about sound and about the process of design. By listening to each other and asking questions, students will have the opportunity to broaden and refine their own understanding and to make additional connections among the investigations in this unit. In addition, this culminating activity will enable you and your students to assess their growth with the skills of recording, interpreting, and communicating results of investigations.

- Students apply their plans to complete their projects.

- Students test and improve the design of their instruments or devices.

- Students make presentations to describe and explain what they have constructed.

Background

Assessing students' ideas and abilities is a challenging and ongoing task, ideally involving many perspectives. The activities in this lesson are both a creative experience for students and an opportunity for you to assess what they know and can do. Students can demonstrate an understanding of sound by explaining how sound is produced (by the vibrating part of their device), how the pitch can be changed, and how the volume can be made louder or softer. Additional suggestions for assessment are included in the post-unit assessment.

Materials

For each student
- 1 completed copy of **Record Sheet 15-A: Design Sheet**
- 1 completed copy of **Record Sheet 15-B: Presentation Planning Sheet**
  Collection of materials provided by you and the students

Preparation

1. Gather any additional materials identified by students in Lesson 15, such as empty containers (for example, milk cartons, plastic trays, clay flowerpots) and pieces of cardboard and string.

2. If students will be making their presentations to another class or to an audience of visitors, arrange a time and suitable room. You may also want to make arrangements to have the presentations videotaped so that students can review them.

Procedure

1. Ask students to review the designs for their instruments or devices from **Record Sheet 15-A** and their presentation plans from **Record Sheet 15-B.** Encourage them to talk with one another about their plans.

2. Encourage students to test their inventions. Challenge them to discuss with their group members possible improvements and modifications to their instruments or devices.

Figure 16-1

Working on a project

3. Remind students that they will be presenting their projects to the class. Have them select who from the group will make the presentation. Discuss their time limits and the process that you want them to follow.

4. Ask students to clean up their work areas as they complete their projects and get ready to make their presentations.

Final Activities

1. Have each group present to the class the instruments or other project that the group planned and carried out. If a group constructed an instrument or a device, ask students to include its name, how it works, and what it is used for, as recorded on their Design Sheet. Also ask them to mention anything they learned in constructing their inventions and any changes they made in their plans. **Record Sheet 15-B** will help them make their presentations.

2. Encourage other students to ask questions about the projects.

Figure 16-2

Making a
presentation

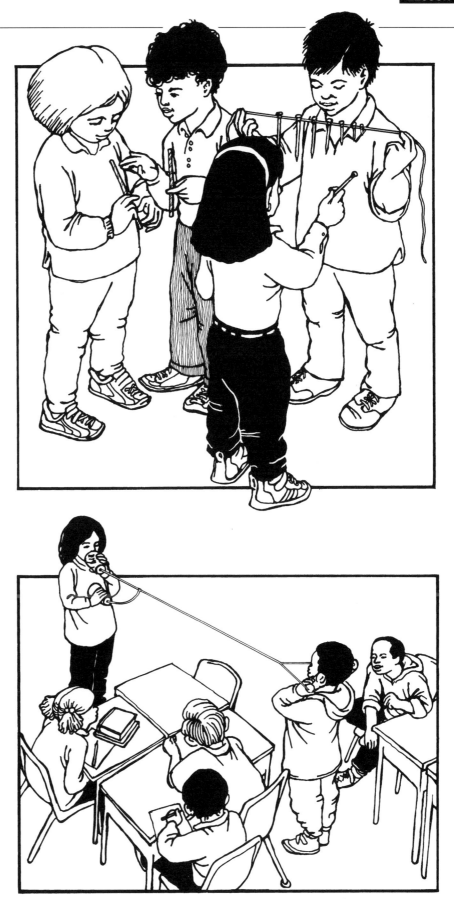

Extensions

SCIENCE

1. Arrange to have students' projects displayed for others in the school to test.

SOCIAL STUDIES

2. Challenge students to create an advertisement to sell their instrument or device. The ad should include the cost of the instrument or device and information about why a person would need or want to buy it.

Assessment

This lesson concludes the two-part assessment in which students applied what they had learned throughout the unit to plan, design, and create an instrument or device. Your observations of their work, as well as students' answers to your questions, will already have provided evidence of how well they understood and applied the major concepts of this unit. The instruments or devices, plans created, and the written descriptions provide hard data that you can use to document learning and the ability to apply that learning to a new situation.

In addition, consider the following when assessing students' growth in understanding during this lesson.

■ Did students follow the plans they developed? Did they modify their plans?

■ What *new concepts* did students learn by constructing their instruments or devices and making their presentations?

■ Do students understand how to change the pitch or volume of sound?

■ Can students articulate their ideas about sound and how it is produced?

Post-Unit Assessment

The post-unit assessment on pgs. 127–28 is a matched follow-up to the pre-unit assessment in Lesson 1. By comparing students' pre- and post-unit responses, you will be able to document their growth in knowledge about sound.

Additional Assessments

Additional assessments for this unit are provided on pgs. 129–32.

Overview

This post-unit assessment of students' ideas about sound is matched to the pre-unit assessment in Lesson 1. By comparing the individual and class responses from these activities, you will be able to document students' learning. During the first lesson, students developed three class charts: "Sounds We Have Heard," "Ways to Make Sounds," and "Questions We Have about Sound." When students revisit these activities, they may better realize how much they have learned about sound, about how sound is produced, and about how the pitch and volume of sounds can be changed.

Materials

For each student
   1   science notebook

For every four students
   1   large tuning fork
   1   small tuning fork

For the class
   3   sheets of newsprint
   1   marker
       Masking tape
       Class charts from Lesson 1: "Sounds We Have Heard," "Ways to Make Sounds," and "Questions We Have about Sound."

Preparation

1. Label one sheet of newsprint "Sounds We Have Heard,"another "Ways to Make Sounds," and a third "Questions We Still Have." Date the sheets and post them where they can be seen easily.

2. Have the class charts by the same titles from Lesson 1 ready to display, but not yet posted.

Procedure

1. Ask students to think about what they have learned in this unit. Then ask them to write in their science notebooks what they now know about sounds they have heard and what they know about ways to make sounds. When you compare these entries with those from Lesson 1, look for new ideas as well as for indications that students' existing ideas have been refined.

2. Display the first two class charts from Lesson 1 ("Sounds We Have Heard" and "Ways to Make Sounds"). Ask students to identify ideas they now know to be true. What experiences did they have during the unit that confirmed these statements?

3. Ask students to look at the charts again and to point out statements they would like to correct, improve, or delete. Remind them to support these suggestions with experiences from the unit.

4. Now ask students to share new information they gained from the unit. What else have they learned?

5. Display the chart "Questions We Have about Sound" from Lesson 1. Ask students what questions on the chart they can now answer. Record any new questions that students have on the new chart, "Questions We Still Have." What are some ways to find out the answers to questions that have not yet been answered? Encourage the class to go on looking for the answers to these questions.

6. Distribute the tuning forks and allow students time to repeat the investigations from Lesson 1.

7. Before they record their results, encourage them to review what they wrote in their notebooks. Ask them to answer the following questions:

   ■ How were the sounds of the tuning forks alike? How were they different?

   ■ How would you describe the sound of the smaller tuning fork? The larger one?

   ■ What did the tuning forks feel like when they made a sound?

Additional Assessments

Overview

Following are some suggestions for assessment activities. Although it is not essential to do all of the suggested assessments, it is recommended that students do Assessment 1.

- Assessment 1 is a questionnaire that students can use to evaluate themselves.

- Assessment 2 is a review of the science notebooks, drawings, record sheets, and other products created during the unit.

- Assessment 3 gives you an opportunity to meet with students individually and to assess their responses to questions concerning sound.

Assessment 1: Student Self-Assessment

Using the questionnaire, students assess their own learning and participation during this unit. Teachers have found it useful to meet with each student individually to discuss the self-assessment. Such meetings give you the opportunity to provide your feedback about the student's work and to compare it with the student's perceptions.

Materials

For each student
   1 **Student Self-Assessment** (on pgs. 131–32)

Procedure

1. Distribute a copy of the **Student Self-Assessment** to each student. Preview it with the class. Explain to the students that it is important to take time to think about how they are working.

2. Allow students time to complete the self-assessment during class, or ask them to complete it as a homework assignment.

Assessment 2: Student Work

Materials

Collection of individual work products, including science notebooks, drawings, record sheets, and any other work products created during the unit.

Procedure

Assemble each student's work. As you review it, remember that third-graders' writing may not reflect the depth and breadth of their knowledge. Nevertheless, third-grade written work can provide information about a student's progress. Consider the following:

- How complete is each product?

- Do the products indicate effort on the student's part?

- Which activities were hardest for the student to do? Which concepts were most difficult to grasp? Which were easiest?

- Do the products reflect growth in the students' knowledge, skills, and understanding?

Assessment 3: Individual Student Meetings

Procedure

This assessment strategy is most effective with students for whom you do not have sufficient evaluation data recorded. Allow time to meet with students individually. Either tape record or write their responses. Use questions from the post-unit assessment as well as additional questions such as these:

- How do we hear sounds?

- How do your vocal cords produce sounds?

- Suppose you wanted to show someone what you know about pitch. How would you go about showing and explaining what you have learned?

Sound
Student Self-Assessment

Name: _____

Date: _____

1. Write three things you now know about how sounds are made.

2. Describe three things that can affect the pitch of a sound.

3. What questions do you still have about sound?

4. List the activities that you liked best in *Sound.* Explain why you liked them.

5. Were there any activities in the unit that you did not understand or that confused you? Explain your answer.

Sound
Student Self-Assessment, *continued*   Name: _____

6. How well do you think you and your partner worked together? Give some examples.

7. Take another look at your science notebook. Describe how well you think you recorded your ideas, experiments, and observations.

8. Think about the work you did in this unit. What do you think you did very well?

   What area of your work do you think you can improve on?

9. How do you feel about learning science? Circle the words that apply to you.

   a. Interested   b. Bored   c. Nervous   d. Excited

   e. Confused   f. Successful   g. Relaxed   h. Happy

   i. Now write down at least one word of your own. _____

Bibliography: Resources for Teachers and Students

This Bibliography provides a sampling of books that complement the *Sound* unit. It is divided into the following categories:

- Resources for Teachers

- Resources for Students

These materials come well recommended. They have been favorably reviewed, and teachers have found them useful.

If a book goes out of print or if you seek additional titles, you may wish to consult the following resources.

Appraisal: Science Books for Young People (The Children's Science Book Review Committee, Boston).

> Published quarterly, this periodical reviews new science books available for young people. Each book is reviewed by a librarian and by a scientist. The Children's Science Book Review Committee is sponsored by the Science Education Department of Boston University's School of Education and the New England Roundtable of Children's Librarians.

Gath, Tracy, and Maria Sosa, eds. *Science Books & Films' Best Books for Children, 1992–1995.* Washington, DC: American Association for the Advancement of Science, 1996.

> This volume, part of a continuing series, is a compilation of the most highly rated science books that have been reviewed recently in the periodical *Science Books & Films.*

National Science Resources Center. *Resources for Teaching Elementary School Science.* Washington, DC: National Academy Press, 1996.

> This guide provides extensive information about some 350 hands-on, inquiry-centered science curriculum materials for grades K–6. It also annotates other published materials—books on teaching science, science book lists, and periodicals for teachers and students. The guide includes annotated listings of museums and federal and professional organizations throughout the country with programs and other resources to assist in the teaching of elementary school science.

Science and Children (National Science Teachers Association, Arlington, VA).

> Each March, this monthly periodical provides an annotated bibliography of outstanding science trade books primarily for elementary students.

Science Books & Films (American Association for the Advancement of Science, Washington, DC).

> Published nine times a year, this periodical offers critical reviews of a wide range of new science materials, from books to audiovisual materials to electronic resources. The reviews are primarily written by scientists and science educators. *Science Books & Films* is useful for librarians, media specialists, curriculum supervisors, science teachers, and others responsible for recommending and purchasing scientific materials.

Scientific American (Scientific American, Inc., New York).

> Each December, this monthly periodical compiles and reviews a selection of outstanding new science books for children.

Resources for Teachers

Dishon, Dee, and Wilson O'Leary. *A Guidebook for Cooperative Learning: Techniques for Creating More Effective Schools.* Holmes Beach, FL: Learning Publications, 1984.

> This practical guide helps teachers implement cooperative learning in the classroom.

Johnson, David W., Roger T. Johnson, and Edythe Johnson Holubec. *Circles of Learning: Cooperation in the Classroom.* Alexandria, VA: Association for Supervision and Curriculum Development, 1984.

> This book presents the case for cooperative learning in a concise and readable form. It reviews the research, outlines implementation strategies, and answers many questions.

Wilson, Frank R. *Tone Deaf and All Thumbs? An Invitation to Music-Making for Late Bloomers and Non-prodigies.* New York: Viking Penguin, 1986.

> Recommended by the Music Educators Conference, this book describes ways to make and enjoy music. According to the author, genuine "tone deafness" is extremely rare, and in most instances, pitch discrimination can be developed by repeated experiences with sounds.

Resources for Students

Ancona, George, and Mary Beth Miller. *Handtalk Zoo.* New York: Macmillan, 1989.

> In this collection of photographs, children visiting the zoo form sign language words as they look at the animals, eat lunch, and head home.

Ardley, Neil. *Music.* Eyewitness Books. New York: Knopf, 1989.

> Text and hundreds of photographs introduce musical instruments from early times to the present. The instruments range from pipes and flutes to electronic synthesizers.

Berger, Melvin. *The Science of Music.* New York: HarperCollins, 1989.

This book discusses important concepts related to sound—pitch, volume, and how people speak and hear—and provides information about musical instruments.

Davidson, Margaret. *Helen Keller.* New York: Bantam Doubleday Dell, 1969.

This biography focuses on the childhood of Helen Keller, who overcame the handicaps of being blind and deaf.

Hausherr, Rosmarie. *What Instrument Is This?* New York: Scholastic, 1992.

Photographs and text introduce students to 16 different musical instruments in the wind, string, keyboard, and percussion instrument groups. The book tells how the instruments sound and the styles of music for which they are best suited. A glossary is included.

Jennings, Terry J. *The Young Scientist Investigates Sounds.* Chicago: Children's Press, 1989.

This book provides descriptions of various sound-related phenomena, including the mechanisms of hearing, speech, and sound production. It contains illustrations and photographs.

Martin, Jr., Bill. *Polar Bear, Polar Bear, What Do You Hear?* Illustrated by Eric Carle. New York: Henry Holt, 1991.

In this picture book, zoo animals such as the polar bear, lion, and walrus make their distinctive sounds for each other, and children imitate the sounds for the zookeeper.

National Institute on Deafness and Other Communication Disorders. *I Love What I Hear.* Video. Bethesda, MD: National Institutes of Health, National Institute on Deafness and Other Communication Disorders, 1991.

This 8-minute video on sound and hearing safety was produced for third- through sixth-grade students. A free copy of the video and accompanying 12-page Teacher's Guide is available to schools free of charge. To obtain a copy, call (800) 241-1044, or write to the National Institute on Deafness and Other Communication Disorders, 1 Communication Ave., Bethesda, MD 20892-3456.

Nichol, Barbara. *Beethoven Lives Upstairs: A Tale of Childhood and Genius.* Sound recording. Toronto: The Children's Group, Classical Kids, 1989. U.S. distributor: BMG Music.

Using more than two dozen excerpts from Beethoven's works, this award-winning recording produced by Susan Hammond tells the story of 10-year-old Christoph, who lives downstairs from the composer. (See the next entry for information on the book by the same title.)

———. *Beethoven Lives Upstairs.* Illustrated by Scott Cameron. First American ed.: New York: Orchard Books, 1994.

Based on an award-winning recording (see the preceding entry), this book combines fiction, history, and music. *Beethoven Lives Upstairs* is a story told through the letters that 10-year-old Christoph and his uncle exchange. Christoph shares his house with "Mr. Beethoven," the famous composer who became completely deaf. The letters show how Christoph's feelings for the eccentric boarder change from anger and embarrassment to compassion and admiration.

Payne, Katharine. "Elephant Talk." *National Geographic*, August 1989, pp. 264–77.

This article describes the author's research on elephant calls below the lowest pitch audible to human ears. Elephants use this low-frequency sound, called infrasound, to communicate across distances of several miles. Informative photographs accompany the text.

———. *Elephants Calling.* Face to Face with Science. New York: Crown, 1992.

In this book illustrated with color photographs, the author tells about her discovery that elephants communicate with low-frequency calls that are inaudible to humans.

Showers, Paul. *Ears Are For Hearing.* New York: HarperCollins, 1990.

This well-illustrated discussion of how the process of hearing works includes guidelines for hearing safety.

———. *The Listening Walk.* Illustrated by Aliki. New ed. New York: HarperCollins, 1991.

This picture book shows a little girl and her father taking a quiet walk and identifying the sounds around them.

Taylor, Barbara. *Living with Deafness.* New York: Franklin Watts, 1989.

This book combines illustrations, photographs, and text to explain hearing, deafness, and ear care. It describes how deafness may be caused, how it can be treated, and how individuals cope with it. The book's focus on children makes it particularly accessible to elementary students.

Coping with Hearing Impairments

Hearing is something that most people take for granted, but many people have trouble hearing. To help screen for hearing problems, almost all school systems conduct some sort of hearing test on elementary school children. These tests are successful at determining which students have chronic hearing problems. Such students will have some difficulties working on the *Sound* unit.

Although most of the activities in the unit have a visual and/or tactile component, students with hearing difficulties will not be able to pick up changes in pitch. It is important to be sensitive to this fact so that students with hearing problems are not made to feel deficient.

Problems Confronting Deaf People

Although deaf people have widely varying interests, beliefs, and employment, many share a common culture and language. American Sign Language (ASL) is the primary language used by approximately 100,000 to 500,000 people. It is not a variation of English, but rather a separate, natural language. ASL makes use of hand, arm, and finger movements as well as facial expressions. Several signs and their meanings are shown in Figure 1.

Figure A-1

ASL signs

Two pieces of equipment—television and the telephone—are particularly difficult for deaf people to use. But the addition of closed captions (CC) to television programs has enabled deaf people to read on the screen the words that are being spoken. Unfortunately, not all television shows include this feature. Nonetheless, it has been a long struggle for deaf people to gain some access to the programming that hearing people take for granted.

This is how a CC works. Broadcasters transmit a short string of coded data, along with the picture and audio signal. Television receivers usually are not sensitive to this data (which contains the caption), but with a special decoder attached to the television set, the caption can be decoded and displayed as printed words at the bottom of the screen.

Another device—a teletype, or TTY—combines the function of a telephone with that of a typewriter. By typing messages that are carried over telephone lines to a teletype machine, deaf people can communicate with hearing people over distances.